— JONATHAN DECUIR ·
with Quanesha Moore

YOUR PURPOSE IS THE SOLUTION

HOW TO LIVE WITH THE BIGGER PICTURE IN MIND AND TRANSFORM YOUR LIFE

SESSION INSTITUTE

DEDICATED

To my hero, my mother, who committed her life to seeing the best in others. Thank you for giving me your very best.

To my dad, who exemplified faith in God and hard work; who showed me what it looks like to passionately pursue the vision God gives you until the end. I believe God.

To all the dreamers, visionaries, and purpose pursuers, which includes YOU. No matter where you find yourself in life right now, as long as you're breathing, you have more to give the world.

CONTENTS

YOUR PURPOSE IS THE SOLUTION

HOW TO LIVE WITH THE BIGGER PICTURE IN MIND AND TRANSFORM YOUR LIFE

CHAPTER 1
BOTTOM LINE

"Don't even try, you're not going to get in."

That's what everyone said when I started my junior year at UC Berkeley. I wanted to take Professor Blaustein's Community Development course because of how dynamic and engaging I heard his classes were. He was a well-known, sought-after professor on campus, and chances of experiencing him for myself were slim. Despite the waitlist, I confidently showed up to his class on the first day of the semester. Fortunately, I was able to chat briefly with him after class and he instructed me to come back the next day. I was in!

Early on, I knew I was destined to help people. In high school, my gift of influence and leadership was evident, even though I didn't have a full grasp of it myself. However, during Professor Blaustein's class, I had one of those purpose moments. You know. When it just *feels right*, life *makes sense*, and the thought crosses your mind, *"This is what I'm supposed to be doing."*

By the end of the semester, it was clear to me that impacting people, and changing lives and communities, specifically my community in Pasadena, CA, was not only what I wanted to do, but also the reason I was breathing. Granted, at the time, this was only a glimpse of what I would come to know as my purpose and life's vision, but isn't that how life works? We get glimpses along the way. Those moments where the reason for our existence becomes a little clearer.

So here is a question for you: Why are you breathing? No, really, think about it. **WHY ARE YOU BREATHING?** If you know the answer, how often do you keep it in the forefront of your mind? Do you allow your "why" to guide your actions and decisions? Or maybe your immediate response is, *"I don't know," "I don't have a why,"* or *"I've lost sight of my why."* Maybe you feel like you are kind of wandering through life blindfolded. Whatever your response is, I want you to take the next sentence you read to heart.

If you have breath in your body, you have a purpose. You may not know what it is yet, or believe it, but there is a unique reason you exist. You have something special, specific, and necessary to offer the world. No one is alive to simply take up space, wander aimlessly, or even just enjoy the finest things in life.

Motivational speaker, Les Brown, once said, *"The graveyard is the richest place on earth, because it is here that you will find all the hopes and dreams that were never fulfilled, the books that were never written, the songs that were never sung, the inventions that were never shared, the cures that were never discovered, all because someone was too afraid to take that first step, keep with the problem, or determined to carry out their dream."*

Yes, fear plays a role, but I think the bigger problem is when people don't have a grasp on their purpose or vision that will carry them through the fear, circumstances, and whatever else life may throw their way. Unfortunately, like Mr. Brown alluded to, there's more at stake than just unfulfilled hopes and dreams. The world misses out on answers, inventions, cures, discoveries, and so much more.

I am convinced that for every problem that exists in the world or that will ever exist, there is a solution. It's simple, the solution is you and me. We all have solutions planted on the inside of each one of us, waiting to be discovered, cultivated, and acted on. That is what matters most. We are breathing because our purpose is the solution. Say it with me: **MY PURPOSE IS THE SOLUTION**.

If you think you know what your purpose is and it's not linked to solving a problem, then I challenge you to reevaluate. If you're not spending time trying to discover your purpose or not acting on it, then I challenge you to reevaluate too. Purpose is not about us. It's bigger than us. So, we have to live out our purpose on purpose every day.

Bob Proctor put it this way, *"Your purpose is why you're living, and your vision is how you're going to exe-*

> Purpose is not about us it's bigger than us

cute it." We live out our purpose primarily by having a vision for our lives. Vision can be likened to the puzzle pieces that create a bigger picture or a journey we take to reach a final destination.

Much like purpose, vision is about the kind of impact we intend to have on the world and the legacy we will leave behind. I believe vision is the gift God places in us to keep us connected to our purpose. It's what we dream about, and sadly, what we often don't act on because we struggle to see the bigger picture or we're trying to reach a destination without a plan.

Vision is more practical than people make it out to be. However, like many quotes on this topic, *"You have to believe it before you see it."* In my opinion, before any-one can pursue vision, we have to first acknowledge and accept that our purpose is the solution. Believing that makes way for a clear path ahead. Not easy, not com-fortable, but clear, because purpose acts as an anchor. It keeps us grounded and clear for the journey.

I imagine, like me, you have some sort of vision for your life; who you want to be, what you want to do, and the kinds of things you desire in life. Which is great, but is it connected to purpose? Nothing matters more than you living the life you were destined to live. Are you ready to take charge of your life and start living on purpose?

On this day,_____, I take a per-sonal stand and join thousands of people around the globe, recognizing that because there is breath in my body, I have a purpose. I commit to actively discovering what that pur-pose is, seeking the support and accountability needed to pursue my vision and purposefully living as the gift I was designed to be in the world. I hereby declare

MY PURPOSE IS THE SOLUTION

_____   _____

Signature   Date

CHAPTER 2
THIS IS FOR YOU

Growing up, I watched my mother spend her life serving and helping others in the community. She was multi-talented and the kind of person anyone could talk to. My mother had a gift for connecting with and seeing in others what they could not see in themselves. She taught me how to trust the potential I saw in others and help draw it out before they even realized it themselves. She believed the best about everyone she met, and more often than not, they proved her right. She was the epitome of compassion and mercy personified. She was my personal hero, as she was for many.

If I had to guess, I'd say my mother's purpose was connected to helping people maximize their potential. She was a champion and coach for the underdog, but somewhere along the way, life and circumstances deterred her. She decided to make my sister and I her primary focus.

I believe she lost sight of the bigger picture, or possibly even decided it was no longer worth fighting for. While I am grateful for her love and the legacy she left, I believe she still had more to give to the world.

I wrote this book for people like my mom who feel like life has caused them to lose sight of their vision. Maybe you think you've already given everything you have or it's best to shift your focus and energy elsewhere.

This is for those who feel like they can't seem to break away from self-limiting beliefs, who feel small, inadequate, and maybe even unworthy of their vision. Perhaps you've started pursuing your vision but you're in need of some direction and motivation, this is for you too.

I have realized that our vision is the first thing we sacrifice when life gets challenging. We are more inclined to negotiate what we see or what we say we want because, let's be honest, it is just easier and more comfortable. It's like playing a game of darts. Instead of being committed to hitting the bullseye (our vision), we settle for throwing the dart, drawing a circle around wherever it lands, and saying that was the intended goal. Do you see the difference?

What to Expect

This book is meant to be both inspirational and practical, so don't think you'll just finish this book feeling inspired. No, the hope is that you're motivated and challenged to act. Here's how it should go: discover, map, act, repeat. We should constantly be discovering our purpose and vision, mapping out the plan, and, most importantly, acting on it.

In Part 1, *Corrective Lenses*, I cover the primary tool I use for processing vision, the Vision Continuum. Much like glasses, it is designed to keep us and our vision in proper perspective. We all have a default way of seeing ourselves and the world, but if we're honest, we'll agree that our default typically ends up undermining us, our goals, and even our relationships. This part will focus on helping us see better.

In Part 2, *In Our Own Eyes,* we will take a closer look at the Biblical narrative of the Children of Israel and their journey to the Promised Land. This is the story that shifted everything for me over a decade ago and prompted me to write this book. Maybe you don't believe in God or read scriptures, but I want to encourage you to read this chapter objectively and ask yourself these questions: How am I like the Children of Israel? What part of their story can I relate to? There's so much about their journey to the Promised Land that parallels our own struggles in pursuing our vision.

Lastly, Parts 3 and 4 are all about action. They cover what you need to make a radical shift in your life and how to practically pursue your vision. I have found that many are not willing to do or be committed enough to stay consistent with what I propose in the last couple of chapters. But like the quote says, *"Nothing will change unless you change."* So, if you are okay with your current level and do not desire the next great thing that life has for you, if you're comfortable with settling for mediocrity, unfulfilled purpose, and only seeing your dreams while you're asleep, then this may not be the book for you.

For the willing, open, determined, and committed, here's how you can get the most out of this book - S.T.O.P.

1. **START WITH THE END IN MIND.** Studies show that only 48% of adults finished a whole book in the last year.

I hope that this is not one of the books you start, get busy, and then abandon on your "I need to finish that" list.

I believe the message and tools in this book can change your life for good. As you read, keep in mind why you picked up the book in the first place. You want something new and different for your life. You want to see your vision materialize. Commit a specific amount of time each day to read this book, and you'll be finished before you know it. More importantly, you'll be closer to your vision.

2. BE **TRUTHFUL** with yourself. One of my favorite scenes from the movie *"The Matrix"* is when Neo is given the option to choose between the red pill and the blue pill. Morpheus says to him, *"All I am offering is the truth."* This book acts as a mirror of sorts. If you remain honest with yourself, I believe you'll find some answers you've been searching for. Bryant McGill, a human potential thought leader and international best-selling author, says, *"Real transformation requires real honesty."*

3. BE **OPEN.** For some, my references to scripture and God may be different from what you're used to or believe. I can even imagine how it may hinder how you read this book. Remember, read objectively. Like I said earlier, consider how you relate to what's being said. Regardless of what you believe, you will agree that some core truths apply to every human. I encourage you to be open to loosening your grip on how you relate to yourself and the world. Keep in mind that we're all operating from a limited view.

4. BE **PRESENT** to the process. So much of what you will read and be challenged to do goes against your default way of thinking, being and doing things. So, pay attention to how your mind and body react to what you read. Take note of the thoughts that come to mind and the feelings that arise. Reflect on any

resistance you may feel within and how you choose to respond to it. It's all a gift. Being present as you read will allow you to see what may have been getting in your way in life. If you can see it, then you can change it.

So, all that said, don't just read what's on these pages, live it. Believe in your vision enough to do whatever it takes to see it with your own eyes. Remember there's a world full of problems and your purpose is the solution to at least one.

TAKE A MOMENT TO

When do you commit to finishing this book by?

How do you plan to make that happen?

What do you hope to get out of this book?

What gets in your way when it comes to vision?

CORRECTIVE LENSES

CHAPTER 3

FOR DAILY USE

The strangest thing happened to me shortly after I turned 40. I couldn't clearly see written words anymore. It was like an overnight change no one really prepared me for. So, I did what I knew many people in my predicament would do. I went to the nearest dollar store and got the best readers I could find. Problem solved. At least for a while.

As time went on, my vision worsened, and eventually, I had to see an optometrist. I had my eyes properly examined and was prescribed my first pair of corrective lenses. Somehow, I went from perfectly fine vision to reading glasses to now wearing prescription glasses daily. Is this something I wanted? No. Is it necessary for my vision? Yes, if I want to see things clearly.

Over the years, I have invested a great deal of time, money, and energy in my personal and professional development. Although I achieved and exceeded many of my goals, I found myself feeling like the vision I had for my life was unattainable. There seemed to be a chasm between who I was, what I was doing, and where I desired to be in life. I was proud of my success, but I wasn't content. I knew there was more for me.

However, there were times when life circumstances caused me to pause and think, "Do I really want more?" or "Am I really supposed to pursue that?" Accomplishments and success are great, but sometimes, they can distract us from pursuing our vision. When challenges arise, we may be tempted to settle for what we've already accomplished, what we're good at, or what feels comfortable.

As I reflected on the chasm and tension I was living in, having a vision while also trying to navigate life, I longed for something to help me process it all. I wondered if there was a way that my life experiences could be used as fuel for my vision instead of roadblocks. I tried everything: books, conferences, podcasts, different apps, you name it, but nothing seemed to help long term. So, I decided to ask God for a solution.

One day, while praying, I received what felt like the Holy Grail of vision to me. It wasn't anything like I ever heard or seen before, but just what I needed. As I applied what God gave me to my life, the chasm seemed a little less wide. It felt like putting on my first pair of glasses. I could finally see clearly, and my life's vision didn't seem so far out of reach.

I call it the *Vision Continuum*. It consists of **God, Capacity, Perception, and Accountability**. While each part has its own focus, they are all connected and work together to help us stay on track. In other words, the Vision Continuum is the pair of corrective lenses we must wear daily to keep ourselves, our vision, and this journey in proper perspective. It will bring things to light, challenge our self-imposed limits, and guard against delusion.

As illustrated below, the continuum is moving counter-clockwise. Like the pursuit of vision, the continuum is not linear, but the illustration is an intentional visual reminder to pursue vision.

Sometimes, the pursuit can feel counter to my default way of being, my environment, and even mainstream culture. Perhaps that's been your experience as well. I believe it also illustrates how God operates, contrary to the ways and systems of the world.

———•—•———

Michelangelo once said, *"Every block of stone has a statue inside it, and it is the task of the sculptor to discover it."*

If we allow Him, God will use our vision to chisel away at the person we are right now to become the masterpiece we were destined to be. Let's be honest, it's not just life circumstances that keep us from vision, it's us.

> God will use our vision to chisel away at the person we are right now to become the masterpiece we were destined to be.

It's how we see ourselves and what we think about our worth or our abilities. It's how we judge the world and others around us. It's our unwillingness, at times, to ask for help or be open and teachable. It's how we feel, whether we're inspired or not, happy, energized, or comfortable. We have to work on all of the above and more as we pursue our vision and become a masterpiece.

It was Michelangelo who also said this about a world-renowned piece, *"I saw the angel in the marble and carved until I set him free."*

In the same way, vision will be used to "set us free." That doesn't mean we get to do whatever we want. It means we are no longer held captive by our fears, failures, shortcomings, or any other personal issues that try to get in the way of the abundant, purpose-filled life we are meant to have. We just have to trust the process.

———•———

In a report published by Research and Markets in 2023, researchers found that the self-help industry in the U.S. was worth approximately $41.2 billion dollars. This number is predicted to rise to $81.6 billion dollars by 2032. From online courses to books to articles and retreats, blaring messages remind us of our untapped potential. Every January, we find ourselves re-motivated to pick up the same goals from the previous year, in addition to whatever new ones we excitedly want to add to the list. Unfortunately, our efforts, for the most part, are unsustainable beyond the emotions that prompted us to start.

I stumbled across an article on LinkedIn that noted *80% of New Year's Resolutions fail, most of them by February.*

Stated as the top two reasons stopping us from achieving what we desire are:

1. We don't have a plan.

2. We don't understand on a *"deep level why we operate the way we do."*

The writer proposes the first step for countering this is the realization that *"It's our consciousness that needs to change before our behavior can change."*

Einstein said it this way, *"We cannot solve a problem on the level of consciousness that created it."* So, before trying to put anything else into practice, we must first be willing to shift our thinking. Even the scripture says, *"Be transformed by the renewing of your minds."*

Another way to think about it is to consider this quote T.D. Jakes posted on Facebook in 2015:

> *"It's not enough to work on self-development, you must work on soil development. If you plant good seed in bad soil, it affects the plant's growth."*

Those who garden can attest to the significance of the soil's role in the health of plants. It has to be tilled and watered. Sunlight is needed, weeds have to be managed, and the environment has to be conducive for growth.

It's the same for us. Our vision is the seed and we are the soil. We cannot afford to bypass or undermine the process. We can't say we want a particular vision for our lives without yielding to whatever deep work it requires of us. That's like gardening without expecting to get a little dirty.

In John 15, a chapter all about growth, Jesus says, *"I am the Vine, and my Father is the Gardener."*

He goes on to say that he cuts off branches that bear no fruit, and He prunes the ones that do, so they can grow more. When it comes to vision, managing our growth may require cutting some things off or pruning, so to speak. For example, cutting off unhelpful habits or relationships.

Vision is a gift. The journey may not always feel comfortable and we may not enjoy every aspect of the process, but it's a gift nonetheless. Vision is there to redirect us when life attempts to derail us. Vision helps us to see clearly when we try to convince ourselves that we are doing better or further along than we actually are.

I'm not saying I have the corner on the market when it comes to pursuing vision, but I do believe the Vision Continuum is a unique and proven way to stay inspired, focused, and honest on this journey. The key is daily use, not occasionally when we see fit. It is not meant to be a temporary fix like the reading glasses I bought, but a corrective fix.

The Vision Continuum has, by far, been the most important and supportive resource for me over the last decade. In the following chapters, I'll discuss each part of the continuum in depth.

CHAPTER 4

THE SOURCE OF VISION

On average, we think approximately 60,000 thoughts a day.

In a study on tendencies of the mind, the National Science Foundation reports that 80% of our thoughts are negative and 95% are repetitive. So, what about those outlier thoughts? The ones that suddenly pop into your head that create energy or excitement, and maybe even compel you to act. Simply put, that's called inspiration.

There is no vision without inspiration. Inspiration is both the igniter and fuel for our vision. The question, then, is where does inspiration come from? Is it something we conjure up? Is it found in nature or art? I believe inspiration can be found anywhere, but for me, the source of my vision and inspiration are one and the same: God. He's the start of the

> There is no vision without inspiration

Vision Continuum and who I go to constantly for direction, clarity, creativity, and energy.

As defined, inspiration is a *"sudden, brilliant, creative, or timely idea."* Interestingly enough, in the Greek New Testament, "inspired" is translated to "God-breathed." While some, maybe you, may not be inclined to acknowledge God in any capacity, I challenge you to consider the possibility that inspiration and vision are produced by something greater than and outside of you.

| Inspiration requires movement

Just as quick as a flame can go out if left unstoked, inspiration can dissipate if we don't respond. It requires movement. Think about the last time you were inspired to do something, and you hesitated or delayed to act. What happened? How long did it take before the energy and excitement dwindled? Better yet, as you delayed, how difficult was it to even remember the original idea? I can't tell you how many times I was inspired to do something, and it never happened. All because I didn't move when I needed to.

I recall reading an article about Beyoncé preparing for her 2018 Coachella performance. I read that she didn't sleep for several days as she prepared and when asked how she did it, she simply replied, "I was inspired."

On a different occasion, I was reminded of two particular Bible stories where people were inspired. Elijah outran chariots on foot and Samson killed an entire army with an animal jawbone. From Beyoncé to Elijah, and all the countless stories we could probably find, there is something to notice about the power of inspiration – it produces a supernatural energy to get things done. The key, however, is to move when it comes.

How often do you find yourself hesitating or waiting? Why? Do you wait until the circumstances are right or until you have all the answers and know exactly what to do? Or do you let yourself or other people talk you out of it? There have been times when I talk myself out of an idea. By discouraging myself from pursuing that inspiration, I misdirect all the energy intended to pursue the vision, and inevitably, lose the inspiration.

| Inspiration requires our ability to notice

Most of the time, we don't even notice when we are being inspired. In a brilliant documentary called *The Social Dilemma,* top executives from well-known companies like Google and Facebook share about the impact of social media and the internet. The unstated question of the industry is, *"How much of your life can we get you to give us?"*

Think about your daily routines. From the moment we wake up, we connect to our phones: browse the news, scroll social media, check emails, and so on. Before we know it, our mind is bombarded and buzzing with so much white noise. It's no wonder we don't notice the gentle nudges of inspiration throughout the day.

Research reveals the average American spends about 5.4 hours on their phone each day. However, 13% of millennials and 5% of boomers say that they spend over 12 hours on their phones every day.

That's literally half of the day! In an effort to encourage users to become more aware of their usage and practice self-regulation, Apple created a tool on their devices to track screen time. But let's be honest, how long would you survive sitting quietly without your phone, computer, tablet, or any active screen nearby? Don't get me wrong, inspiration can come from the internet and social media but more often than not, they leave us feeling envious, inadequate, or simply complacent.

Aside from phones and social media, what other things distract you? What gets most of your attention and energy?

| Inspiration requires that we manage energy-snatchers

Recently, I realized that I regularly feel inspired and notice it in time. The only problem is, I often don't have the energy to act. Can you relate? Do you find yourself pulled in so many directions? Work, home, the ups and downs of life, and people frequently snatch our energy away. By the time we actually have the space to pursue our vision, we can't focus.

Sometimes you read a story that you've already read numerous times, but something new sticks out. This happened to me while reading a story from the Gospels. Jesus was in a

> Much like Jesus, we have the ability to manage who and what we give our energy to.

town full of people wanting His attention, on a healing mission for an important man who lived there. While He pushed through a crowd, a woman who needed healing reached out and touched His robe (Luke 8:44). Immediately, He turned around and asked, *"Who touched me?"* Confused, His disciples responded, *"Master, you are standing in the middle of a crowd, there are a lot of people touching you."* Jesus replied, *"Someone touched me. I felt power leave me..."*

In a crowd full of people coming to Jesus for similar reasons, He chose to let that woman receive His healing power. After all, He was Jesus! He had the ability to control His healing. What I realized is, much like Jesus, we have the ability to manage who and what we give our energy to. There will always be a demand for our time and attention. Sometimes, it will feel like we don't have control, but to reach our vision, we have to reserve energy for our deeper priorities. This requires intentional adjustments.

Perhaps it means using the "Do Not Disturb" button while you're working or limiting call lengths. Managing energy-snatchers could also look like setting boundaries with your family and significant other. You have to learn what works for you specifically, and this often requires trial and error. Evaluate the energy-snatchers in your life and determine what to do with them.

| Inspiration requires imagination

Our imagination is one of the greatest resources available to us. It gives us the ability to place our minds in a space where our bodies haven't arrived. Think of it this way, *imagination is rehearsal*. Research has proven that imagination is powerful, for the amazing fact that the brain is unable to distinguish between the mind's imagination and reality. Simply imagining something causes your brain to react like it's real and your body may soon follow. When we worry about something bad happening, our body reacts as though it's actually happening. The same applies to excitement and inspiration. When we feel inspired, we need to harness the power of our imagination. This becomes the catalyst for our vision, and the thing that sustains our execution of the vision. It creates desires, reinvigorates, and ultimately causes action.

Why do Super Bowl advertisers pay $5.25 million or more for a 30-second commercial? That's $175,000 per second! They want to *captivate your imagination*. They know if they succeed, you'll be more likely to buy what they sell. It was noted, *"In past years, ads have made almost as big an impression as the game or half-time show, and plenty of people watch just for the comical commercials. Television viewership for the Super Bowl averaged more than 111 million people over the last five years."*

With the attention of that many people, companies willing to pay the advertisement cost must capture and hold the viewers' interest for the entire commercial spot. Even more so, their real success comes when shoppers purchase their product, all because they tapped into buyers' imagination.

Imagination Has a Shadow Side

Our imagination is an amazing gift but has a shadow side: worry. Worry is the negative, unfruitful use of imagination. It typically leads us to an unfavorable outcome, like a self-fulfilling prophecy. French philosopher Michel De Montaigne once said, *"My life has been full of terrible misfortunes, most of which never happened."*

The article goes on to talk about a study designed to look into how many of

> Worry is the negative, unfruitful use of imagination.

our imagined calamities never materialize, and they discovered that 85% of what people worried about never happened. That's worth saying again: 85% OF IT NEVER HAPPENED!

When it comes to our vision, worry reflects the anticipation of failure. This causes us to live in the emotion of a failure that hasn't even happened. Unlike the positive impact of imagination and the movement it provokes, worry does the opposite. It strangles the life out of our vision and paralyzes us.

———•———

Worry causes a terrible case of the "what ifs." *"What if I don't make any money?" "What if no one likes what I produce?" "What if I'm not good enough?"* What if, what if, what if. Scientifically speaking, the stress hormones that worry dumps into our brains have been linked to shrinking brain mass, lowered IQ, depression, and other negative effects. So, if you feel stuck, maybe it's because worry has hijacked the energy you need for creativity and action.

Remember, inspiration is a gift from God to fuel our vision. The moment we receive inspiration, we also receive responsibility. We have to make moves, manage distractions, exercise our imagination, and be mindful of worry. Like everything we will discuss in the book, this will require practice, consistency and discipline. We must develop the capacity to respond properly to inspiration as it comes. We must also remember that we're human and that God is God. If we miss an opportunity or fail in some way, we can be assured there's more coming to be prepared for.

TAKE A MOMENT TO

When do you commit to finishing this book by?

How do you plan to make that happen?

What do you hope to get out of this book?

What gets in your way when it comes to vision?

On the left side, write down all the things you find your-self worrying about. This can be connected to your vision and future and everyday life. On the right side, write down your vision and everything you say you want.

WORRY   **VISION**

How much energy do you spend worrying about the things above? (Out of 100%) Write it in the box

100 - the percent of energy used worrying = the amount of energy left for your vision

CHAPTER 5
CAPACITY MATTERS

Picture trying to fit the Pacific Ocean in a 16 oz water bottle. No matter what you believe or try to do, the bottle is only going to hold 16 ounces. The container has to be bigger if the aim is to hold anything more. It's simple: more capacity is required if more is desired.

It's the same with us and our vision. A mentor once told me, *"If you want more, you have to become more."* That said, capacity is our ability and willingness to grow as our vision requires. It involves expanding by learning new information or skill and putting it into practice in our lives. Since vision is often bigger than we find ourselves able to handle, our capacity has to be constantly measured and expanded. I'm sure you

> Capacity is our ability and willingness to grow as our vision requires.

would attest to the fact that vision doesn't magically happen overnight.

Take Jesus as an example. Even he had to grow, whether you see him as a great historical figure or the Son of God. The scripture says as Jesus was maturing, *"He grew in wisdom and stature, and favor with both God and man."*[1] He wasn't born performing miracles and impacting towns.

Similarly, David was called to be king as a young boy, but it took nearly 20 years before he actually took the throne. In the beginning, he was just a shepherd boy. He had to learn, mature, and sometimes fight for his life. Then he became king, later deemed one of the most well-known figures in Jewish history.

If Jesus and King David had to grow into who they were destined to be, why do we think we don't? Whether we like it or not, there is a gap between the picture we have in our mind and our current reality. It's easy to look at successful people every day, admiring or envying where they are, without processing what it took for them to get there and what it takes for them to stay there. Let's take Oprah, for example, a household name now, but many don't know that seven months into being on nighttime news, she was fired and told that she was "unfit for television news." She continued to work, learn, and grow and, shortly after, was given the opportunity for a daytime television segment. The rest is history. Oprah once said, *"No experience is wasted.*

Everything in life is happening to grow you up, to fill you up, to help you become more of who you were created to be."

———•———

Several years ago, I spent time leading personal development and leadership training for youths and young adults in Los Angeles. One of the tools I used in my training, *Strategies for Inside Change*, was the Four Stages of Competence. It was taken from the Conscious Competence Learning Model, which was developed to manage awareness and measure skill level. One must be open, teachable, and diligent when trying to reach a goal. When it comes to vision, this model can be used to determine what new information or skill is needed, where you are in the journey, and what's required for forward movement.

Essentially, when someone is open to learning something new, they must progress through four psychological levels before reaching a level of mastery.

Let's look at it:[2]

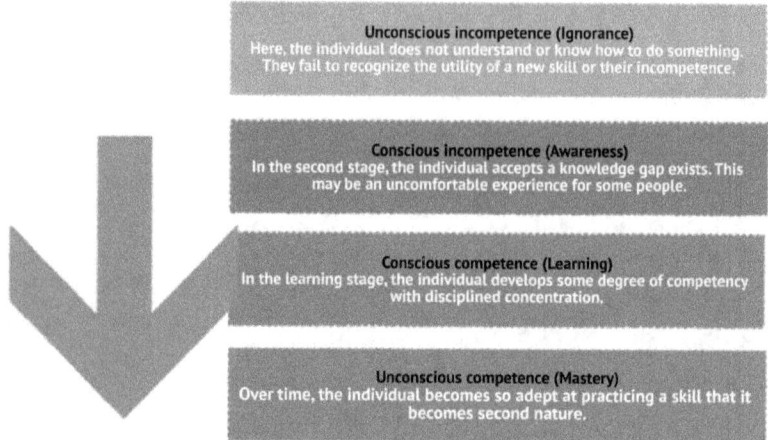

Unconscious incompetence (Ignorance)
Here, the individual does not understand or know how to do something.
They fail to recognize the utility of a new skill or their incompetence.

Conscious incompetence (Awareness)
In the second stage, the individual accepts a knowledge gap exists. This
may be an uncomfortable experience for some people.

Conscious competence (Learning)
In the learning stage, the individual develops some degree of competency
with disciplined concentration.

Unconscious competence (Mastery)
Over time, the individual becomes so adept at practicing a skill that it
becomes second nature.

Unconscious Incompetence

You don't know what you don't know. In this stage, we are completely blind to the fact that we don't know something that is needed or could be supportive of our vision. If we are not open to the fact that we don't know everything, then we will potentially stay where we are. One of the fundamental reasons for failure is because one does not even know they lack the skills to succeed.

Over the years, I've mentored tons of people, young and old. One of the top lessons I teach everyone I mentor is to be teachable. You can't let what you think you know keep you from learning what you need to know. Whenever someone says, "Oh, I know...," my response is typically, "*To know and not do is to not know.*"[3] If we are not teachable and willing to learn anything new, then it's likely our vision will be stalled.

Conscious Incompetence

You know what you don't know. This is a step in the right direction because now we can see and take responsibility for our own growth. At this stage, people are tempted to remain ignorant, or at least pretend to be, because it's clear that growth requires effort. Not only does it require effort, but more often than not, we will have to ask for help. This is where collaboration, mentorship, coaching, and things like therapy, trainings, conferences and so on come in. Conscious Incompetence is a launching pad towards your vision. Billionaire Ray Dalio once said, *"Success comes from knowing what you don't know, more than knowing what you do know."* [4]

Conscious Competence

After investing time and dedication to learning a specific skill or information, you now know what you know. This is all about incorporating what you've learned into your daily life and vision. Renowned author Malcolm Gladwell popularized the 10,000-hour rule[5]. He stated that *"10,000 hours is the magic number of greatness."* Anyone who puts that much time into practicing anything will surely become great at it.

I'm not proposing you spend 10,000 hours doing anything, but could you imagine what your life would look like if you did. That amount of time equates to a little over a year, so it's not out of reach. Reaching this level of competency just requires commitment and consistency. Remember, vision does not happen overnight.

Unconscious Competence

As you constantly make these adjustments, it will impact who you are and how you show up in the world. You become closer to the kind of person who can live out their vision and sustain it along the way. In this stage, your new skill is mastered, and you operate with little to no effort. The move from conscious competence to unconscious competence is like learning to drive. You start off apprehensive and careful of your every move. But before you know it, you begin to drive with ease, sometimes while mindlessly doing other things. To be clear, we will always be learning and growing. Ralph Waldo Emerson said, *"Unless you try to do something beyond what you have mastered, you will never grow."*

When you process the four levels of competence, capacity means doing what Emerson said: Going beyond what you have already mastered. The reality is there will always be something for us to learn and ways in which we can grow when it comes to our purpose and vision. This is just a model that can be used to process how teachable you are and your level of commitment and competency.

———•———

It is important to note that there is a difference between vision and fantasy. It's fantasy to believe there's a container big enough to hold the Pacific Ocean. Sometimes, people can say they have a vision, and attempt to build capacity for something that is really fantasy. How many times have you seen people on shows like American Idol who have a vision of becoming the next winner, but can't sing? Their vision may feel real to them, but you can't build on something that has no foundation. You need to have the capacity for your vision. Building capacity is connected to something that can be learned and attained for a vision that's actually real.

My Battle with Capacity

In 2018, I was inspired to host my first conference called The Blueprint Conference. It was curated for people who want to be inspired, discover their purpose and pursue their dreams. At the time, I had 13 years of experience coaching people around vision and purpose. I also had tons of experience hosting smaller events, seminars, and trainings alike. I felt like I was fully equipped and ready to do something of this magnitude.

So, I gathered my team, invited some of my most influential, and successful friends as guest speakers, and began to promote it. To my surprise, the response from my network was unfavorable. While there were over one hundred people in attendance, and the impact of the conference changed people's lives, it simply didn't yield the results I expected. I was devastated.

The way I interpreted the lack of attendance was people didn't have the same assessment of the conference's value as I did. I priced the conference at the amount I believed it was worth without even considering aspects of hosting and promoting that I didn't know. *I didn't know what I didn't know.*

It wasn't until I prayed and talked to my best friend, Ray Murray, that I realized I had attempted to do something not only beyond my capacity but beyond the capacity of my team. While it appeared to be a decent number in attendance, the reality was I paid for more than half of them to be there. My reach for something higher than God told me ended up costing me more in the end. The problem wasn't that I did the conference, it was that I was trying to do it beyond my level of competency and beyond the vision of what God initially gave me.

Part of the reason I charged the amount I did for registration is because I thought I was at that level where I could. I'm not saying I wasn't worth it, I'm just saying I had not built to the level where others knew it would be worth it to them. In part, capacity is about proof. What is the fruit or evidence of the time you have put in? If your vision has anything to do with other people, then more often than not, they are going to want some proof before they buy in.

Shortly after the conference, I attended a transformational training hosted by GAP Community.[6] In this particular training, they said feedback is neither positive or negative, it's neutral. Up until then, I had taken the lack of attendance at my conference as negative feedback about my capacity. I took it personal, like most people. We have a tendency to attach deep personal meaning to feedback, which is a sign that we have connected what we do to our identity. If the feedback is negative, then our resolve sometimes is that we are not good enough, which, of course, is not true. Feedback is essential for capacity because it is a primary way to know whether we're on track toward our vision or not. It keeps us grounded in reality and guards against delusion.

If I had taken the time to assess where I was, I would have made different decisions based on my capacity then. Nearly two years later, I hosted another conference that yielded greater results all around. I didn't allow the feedback from the previous conference to discourage me from hosting another, but rather, I used it to own where I failed, seek counsel, further develop myself and my team and do the next conference much better.

———•———

Behind the scenes

Much of capacity building is behind-the-scenes work. It's all the time, energy, and effort that no one sees that leads to success and the kind of character needed to sustain it. When I think of my success, I'm reminded of David and his victory against Goliath. People often praise David's courage, strength, and boldness to defeat a giant without really taking into account all the small victories he already won. He fought lions, killed bears, shepherded sheep, and even served lunch to those fighting in battle. Everything he did behind the scenes shaped him for his great victory in front of everyone else. That's to say, don't dismiss or be discouraged by your behind-the-scenes victories. They will shape you if you let them.

Businessman and writer Max DePree said, "*We cannot become what we want by remaining what we are.*" When it comes to vision, capacity matters. If we are not willing to access where we are, be open to learning, and put in some work, then our vision will always be a distance away. We'll be tempted to blame others, our circumstances, or even resolve that it just wasn't meant to be, but ultimately, we are responsible for doing whatever it takes to make our vison happen.

TAKE A MOMENT TO

What's something you could put into practice this week that would support you and your vision?

What is some feedback you received that you perceived as negative or took personally? How could you reframe it?

Any other thoughts on capacity?

CHAPTER 6
PERCEPTION IS KEY

Perception is the key. It is either going to lock us in a prison or allow us to freely live out our purpose and vision. Everyone quotes the infamous saying, *"Perception is reality."* Meaning if you perceive something, then it might as well be that, even if it's not. Perception is a lens through which reality is viewed, not necessarily reality itself.[7]

This is significant, especially when it comes to vision, because our self-perception impacts everything we do, and how we choose to show up in the world. We can be inspired, we can build capacity, but if our perception is misaligned, then we will be stuck. Hence, why I said it is the key that could lock us in a prison. We can become captives by our own view of self, even if it's not true. There's a quote by Stephen Richards that says, *"What we perceive about ourselves is greatly a reflection of how we will end up living our lives."* [8]

Perception is different from perspective: perspective is what you see, while perception is what you interpret. Have you ever had an experience where it seems like other people see something in you that you can't see yourself? That's not because the object of what you're looking at is different. It's how you perceive it. It's the same as someone viewing the glass as half empty or half full.

According to the etymology dictionary, perception means to *"thoroughly grasp, take, or embrace."* It is subjective and typically influenced by our environment and experiences. Much of what we learn from those two becomes the truth we live by, which is no problem, except when it gets in the way of vision.

In a course I teach on vision, I outline the 3 truths that impact our perception. It was adapted, in part, from Neil DeGrasse Tyson's theory on truth.[9] There is systematic truth, which includes beliefs reinforced through culture and institutions. There is personal or experiential truth, which is true to us simply because we believe it on a deep level. It's true because it's connected to an experience we had. Lastly, there is objective truth, which they say is true regardless of if you believe it. For Tyson, this would be something that's been proven by science or a universal principle, like gravity.

In contrast to Tyson's definition of objective truth, I consider The Truth, which is God's Word. Regardless of whether we believe it or not, God's Word is true and trust-worthy. Understanding the difference between the three, as it relates to perception, is important because if we live only according to systematic and experiential truth, we miss out on an abundance of resources available through The Truth.

There's a story in scripture where the Prophet Elisha and the city of Dothan found themselves surrounded by a massive army from the North. Upon seeing the army, one of Elisha's servants started to panic. So, Elisha prayed, *"O Lord, please open his eyes that he may see"* because what Elisha saw was more helpful. The servant perceived they were outnumbered, but the truth was that there was a vast, angelic army surrounding Dothan, ready to fight for them. If the servant was open to the Truth that God was with them over his experience of the army He could see, his response may have been different.

Look at it this way: you may hold a deep belief that you're not qualified to do something due to something you were told when you were young. Perhaps this unhelp-ful belief was reinforced by experiences or other people and you choose to just accept it as the truth. What many people don't realize, or exercise is their power to choose something different. We can choose the Truth of what God says about us over other things we believe to be true about us.

In simple terms, our human tendency to seek out and accept ideas that fit pre-existing beliefs while also easily rejecting information that doesn't fit is called cognitive bias. Even if it's not true and works against the vision we have for our lives, we are more willing to believe the bias over something that would be beneficial to us or is The Truth about us. My business partner often says this quote she heard, *"Belief is stronger than the truth unless you believe truth."*

Take a look at this illustration:

These are the three truths, but the Truth stands alone. We get to filter through our experiences and environments and separate the "trash" before accepting it as a belief. Remember, what we believe to be true impacts how we see ourselves and our vision.

Another root definition of perception is *"percievor,"* which means to obtain, collect, and occupy. We are responsible for what occupies our minds. We have the choice to choose. The moment we decide to change our perceptions will be the same moment we start to experience a change in our reality.

When it comes to vision, our perception of ourselves, most importantly, of our vision and others, must constantly be evaluated and redirected if needed. Perception can truly make or break vision. As we will see with the Children of Israel, how they perceived themselves and the situation they were in cost them greatly — it took them another 40 years to get to the Promised Land. How long do you want to miss out on your vision? How much money are you willing to lose? Or whatever else your current state of perception may be costing you.

TAKE A MOMENT TO

Write down all the words that come to mind when you think about yourself. What do you think others think about you?

What are some thoughts you need to throw away?

CHAPTER 7
ACCOUNT- ABILITY

It seems like we live in a time where accountability has become more highlighted in culture than ever. You can hire an accountability coach or join an accountability group. If you commit to a diet or workout plan, you may be told it's best to have an accountability partner. On the news, we're seeing more and more people being exposed and held accountable for their actions. No one is above the law, as it should be. However, it does seem like accountability has just become one of those buzzwords that people either love or hate. Feelings aside, it is valuable, but when it comes to vision, I want to offer a deeper perspective than the norm.

After looking at the etymology of the word, I gained a new revelation that shifted my relationship with accountability. "Account" means to count, reckon, or explain. It's further explained as one reckoning or giving a detailed explanation of the account/money they've been trusted with. "Ability," when broken down into "able" –"ilty" means the condition or quality or being able, capable of, or even required in some uses.

As I reflected on that, I realized that account-ability is more than someone checking on you or checking off a list of to-dos. It's a posture of the heart. It's having the mind to understand that the vision I've been given doesn't actually belong to me. It's like an account I've been entrusted to manage. I get to figure out what to do with it, how to invest it, make it grow, sustain it, and ultimately account for it one day.

So, I define account-ability as the willingness and ability to steward the vision God gave you through intentionality and partnership. If I choose to operate from the space of stewardship and not ownership, that reduces the temptation to treat my vision however I like. Stephen Covey put it this way, *"Accountability breeds responsibility."* I am responsible for knowing and doing what's needed to see the vision materialize. Accountability is like the cousin to capacity. Just because you're responsible for

> Account-ability as the willingness and ability to steward the vision God gave you through intentionality and partnership.

the account now doesn't mean you have to know it all or have all the things needed right now. Being accountable requires both intentionality and, in many cases, partnership with other people.

| Intentionality

If you haven't noticed by now, I'm big on words and their meanings. Intentionality at its root is connected to both having intent or purpose and exerting effort.[10] This is where developing habits, being disciplined, taking ownership of your actions, and following through on your word come into play. Which then ties accountability to integrity. Not just, *am I going to do the right thing when no one is looking?* But also, *am I going to consider all parts at play?*

By definition, integrity means whole or integrated. So, when we talk about vision and accountability, it's crucial that we consider all the key aspects of our life, mental, emotional, physical, financial, and spiritual, and practice operating from an integrated space versus a divided one. What I've seen is people focus on one or two aspects, like finances or spirituality, while neglecting their physical and mental health, as if they don't matter. I've been guilty of doing it too and the problem I've witnessed is sooner or later, the areas that are being neglected end up demanding attention, sometimes jeopardizing the vision altogether.

That's why I advocate for harmony over balance, figuring out how to live in such a way where all parts are at play, which takes us back to intentionality.

| Partnership

Partnership in accountability is vital because we have a natural inclination to compromise when things are difficult or unclear. Compromise makes way for partial commitment, but partnership can help bridge the gap. When we partner with someone, be it a mentor, a coach, or an accountability group, we receive the support and resources we would not have otherwise. Bob Proctor, an inspiring motivational speaker and author, once said, *"Accountability is the glue that ties commitment to results."* Partnering with others only makes the glue stronger. We also manage or cut down on time and energy when doing it with someone who's already been where we're headed because we're not doing it alone.

Sometimes, people collapse accountability with rebuke or make it mean something personal about their identity or competence, but accountability is a gift. There's a proverb that says, *"Whoever loves instruction and discipline loves knowledge, but he who hates reproof and correction is a fool"*[11]. Accountability is not about being called out, you're being called forward. It propels you to the next level.

Resistance to accountability is a signal that something is at stake: our ego, our comfort, or a desire to be in control, or look good. We must keep this in the forefront of our minds: vision is not about us, nor is it for us. We are simply stewards and beneficiaries of vision and should treat it as such.

> Resistance to
> accountability is a
> signal that something
> is at stake

TAKE A MOMENT TO

Up until now, how have you holding your vision? How well have you been stewarding it?

Which areas of your life have you been neglecting? How can you be more intentional?

Where in your life would partnership be helpful?

IN OUR OWN EYES

CHAPTER 8

IN OUR OWN EYES

"But the men who had gone up with him [Caleb] said, 'We can't attack those people; they are stronger than we are.' And they spread among the Israelites a bad report about the land they had explored. They said, '... all the people we saw there are of great size'. We seemed like grasshoppers in our own eyes, and we looked the same to them."

~ Numbers 13:31-33

The Children of Israel had been wandering in the wilderness for two years. God instructed their leader Moses to send a leader from the twelve tribes to spy on a land. This wasn't just any land, but one that was said to be beautiful and bountiful, "flowing with milk and honey," and, more importantly, a land that was meant to be *theirs*. After surveying the land and seeing that it was occupied, the twelve spies returned to the wilderness and ten of them proclaimed, *"We seemed like grasshoppers in our* own *eyes."* This negative report spread among the Children of Israel and their pursuit of the Promised Land was halted, solely because of their perception.

When it comes to vision, our own self-perception will often hinder our pursuit. We can't be so quick to question and point the finger at the Children of Israel, or anyone else for that matter, without first processing how we seem *in our own eyes*. Maybe we wouldn't call ourselves grasshoppers, but I'm sure we can all attest to feeling small, incapable, and even unworthy at some point on this journey. This small self-view causes us to stop pursuing our own vision and purpose. I call this the **Grasshopper Complex**.

If you remember from the Vision Continuum, we discussed that perception is connected to what we embrace about ourselves and our experiences. It's not just the events of life, but our interpretation of them that counts. While ten of the spies had negative reports, the other two spies told the Children of Israel that they could, in fact, overtake the inhabitants and enjoy the "exceedingly good" land, but the Children of Israel chose to embrace the negative report from the other ten spies. If we look closely at their story, we'll see how life shapes our perception, which, if unaddressed, can hinder us from experiencing the greatness of our vision and purpose.

A Glimpse of the Promise

Way before the Children of Israel even existed, God promised Abraham that he would be the father of many nations. His descendants, God said, would number greater than the grains of sand and they would inhabit the wonderful land of Canaan. The thing was, he and his wife Sarah were childless and beyond childbearing years when this prophesy was given, but they had faith in God and eventually birthed a son named Isaac. Abraham and his family settled in Canaan just like God promised. Fast-forward two generations. Abraham's grandson Jacob, aka Israel, had twelve sons that would become the twelve tribes of Israel. Abraham's descendants were multiplying and prospering in the Promised Land. The Children of Israel were living the good life! They were favored by God and living in the Promised Land. What more could they have wanted?

That is, until a terrible famine ravaged the land and Jacob was forced to make a decision. He and his family had to leave Canaan and journey to Egypt to find food. Can you imagine the devastation, the disappointment, and the despair? Their situation shifted unexpectedly.

When we experience unexpected shifts in life, it sometimes causes us to put a pause on our vision. We get a glimpse of what could be and then we're forced to move in a different direction. At the time, we are just doing what we have to do, but I wonder how many people actually process how unexpected life events really impact them. It's not hard for me to imagine people questioning, *Did I make the right decision? Could I have done something else?* or *Will I ever get back to my vision?* Because I've asked those questions myself. As you reflect on your own life, can you identify where some unexpected shifts took place and the impact they had on you?

Trapped by Comfort

After finding refuge and food in Egypt, I'm sure the Children of Israel had no intention of extending their stay, but that's exactly what happened. They were drawn to Egypt out of need but stayed because of *comfort*. What was once a place of refuge gradually transformed into their prison. Now, I'm not out to paint Egypt as some bad place because it isn't. However, for the Children of Israel, it became a place of captivity. As time went on, the people who once welcomed and favored the Children of Israel died and resentment arose among the new generation of Egyptian leaders. They enslaved and horribly oppressed the Children of Israel for 400 years.

I think it's interesting how life can lead us to places that are beneficial for us at one point, but then eventually, we find ourselves trapped. Possibly because we got too comfortable. Sometimes, it's not even our fault. Think about it, the generation of enslaved Israelites was not the same generation that decided to stay in Egypt in the beginning. We can't even fully blame the older generation either because we don't know what they experienced, what they were thinking, and why they made the choices they did. All we know is the Children of Israel were no longer living in the Promised land, but as descendants of Abraham. They were not meant to be slaves. I am inclined to say the same about us. Sometimes we find ourselves at a certain place in life because of the decisions someone else made. However, at the end of the day, we were not meant to be held captive, trapped by our decisions or the decisions of those before us. We are people of vision and purpose and we are meant to pursue it, even if we don't fully know what "it" is just yet.

> We are people of vision and purpose and we are meant to pursue it

The Tension of Transition

God eventually raised Moses to save the Children of Israel. He was young yet admired. He had a great deal of political and social capital. If you're familiar with the story or ever watched a rerun of the old movie *The Ten Commandments,* Moses demanded, *"Let my people go!"*

Though it wasn't immediate, the Children of Israel were eventually released from Egyptian captivity and led into the wilderness.

They had earned their freedom, but they had a difficult transition ahead of them. In Egypt, though enslaved, all of their needs were provided for. Now, they found themselves alone. All they knew was Egypt. They had only heard stories about being descendants of Abraham and heirs of the Promised Land, but they had no real reference for what that meant. They simply couldn't see what they had never seen, but they chose to pursue the Promised Land anyway. However, the tension caused them to complain.

In our pursuit of vision, let's be aware that we will experience tension, especially if you come from a background where you're the first. The first to graduate from college, own a business, or leave home to pursue something greater. Maybe the tension is coming from leaving the comfortable, but like the Children of Israel, your vision is greater than where you were. You just have to be willing to go in faith.

Majority Rules

Now back to where we started, Numbers 13:33, the spies reporting about the land of Canaan. The Children of Israel chose to embrace the report of the majority because that's what they had always done. The majority decided to stay in Egypt, the majority decided to complain in the wilderness, and now, the majority said, *"We are not strong or big enough to possess the Promised Land."* For the Children of Israel, the perception may have been, *"This must be true because our ancestors weren't strong enough to get out of the Egyptian captivity. We also weren't capable of providing for ourselves in the wilderness, so that must mean the Promised Land isn't for us."* The majority shaped their self-perception and if we aren't careful, we'll find ourselves embracing a story that was written by the majority, too.

Sometimes, the majority voice can be found internally. One of my former professors, Dr. Dani, talks about a concept called the "committee of you." Imagine a conference table. At the table sits the different parts of you that have a voice: your inner child, the adult you, the you that always looks out for themselves, the best version of you and whoever else. They all have experiences that have shaped their voice. These inner voices may sometimes join forces to steer us away when we decide to do something different and pursue our vision and dreams. They're like the majority in the Children of Israel's story. They've reasoned that it's better to return to what they know rather than pursue what they are destined for.

CHAPTER 9
WILDERNESS WANDERING

"Forty years spent in wandering in a wilderness like that of the present is not a sad fate – unless one attempts to make himself believe that the wilderness is after all itself the Promised Land."

~ John Dewey

The Children of Israel chose the wilderness over the Promised Land. Some even sought to select a leader that would lead them back to Egypt, back to slavery. Did they fail to see how they could possess the Promised Land, or was there a deeper issue in play? Despite having experienced the faithfulness of God in the wilderness and hearing a good report with supporting evidence about the Promised Land, the Israelites couldn't help but complain and rebel. As a result, they found themselves wandering around in the wilderness again, except, this time, it took much longer before they could experience the promise. Forty more years to be exact.

Wilderness wandering can be likened to the unhealthy cycles we find ourselves in. No matter how much we try to change, we find ourselves caught in loops of self-sabotage, procrastination, and survival strategies that no longer serve us. It's quite possible we aren't even aware of our poor self-perception. The problem is that non-evaluated perceptions can perpetuate unhealthy life cycles and limit possibility.

Perhaps, like the Children of Israel, it's something deeper. There has to be a reason for our "wandering in the wilderness" experience. It's easy to read the fact that the Children of Israel spent 400 years enslaved without really processing the trauma they must have endured. This experience collectively shaped who they were and the decisions they made. The same goes for us. When we live through a traumatic experience or season, and we don't process its impact on our lives, it will affect our decisions. But if we're willing to really look at our stories, we may be able to see how our own trauma keeps us in cycles, ultimately prolonging our journey to vision.

> Non-evaluated perceptions can perpetuate unhealthy life cycles and limit possibility.

Just Trying to Survive

Simply defined, survival is the *state of living or existing, despite an accident, ordeal, or difficult circumstance.* Survival mode is something we were created with in order to preserve our species. Neuroscience claims one of the most important jobs of the brain is to ensure our survival, even under the most miserable conditions. Unfortunately, sometimes, if not most, our brains will continue to operate in survival mode even after the trauma is over. Research proves how complex our brains can be while at the same time blind, so to speak, to key information. For instance, our brains are wired to respond in the face of danger but can't tell the difference between perceived danger and real danger.

So, whether we realize it or not, our brain will respond to external information according to its programming. But trauma can play a huge role in that. It's kind of like a pair of glasses. Trauma is the lens, and how we see the world is determined by the kind of lenses we have on. At some point, the glasses were necessary, but the problem comes when we don't take them off and put on lenses more fitting for our current circumstances. In the book *The Body Keeps Score,* author Bessel van der Kolk notes, *"Being traumatized means to continue to organize your life as if the trauma were still going on as if every encounter or event is contaminated by the past."* Our brain is separated into parts with different functions, and sometimes, the parts don't talk to each other about everything. So, no matter how much our rational brain knows, our emotional brain will kick in when we get triggered. It'll often hijack the situation, placing reason in the back seat. Trauma increases the risk of misinterpreting information, which includes new life experiences and relationships with others.

We saw firsthand how the Children of Israel were so quick to embrace the negative report and perceive themselves as grasshoppers. Well, after being oppressed for 400 years, who wouldn't feel inferior? It's no wonder they felt powerless to overtake anyone. While trauma can happen in a moment or be experienced over a span of time, it is guaranteed to mark our self-perception, which ultimately affects our movement and pursuit of vision.

As neuroscience reports, *"Very few psychological problems are the result of defects in understanding; most originate in pressures from deeper regions in the brain that drive our perception and attention."*[12] This constant state of being driven by one's emotions and impacted by trauma can literally cause someone to feel like they're on the run but getting nowhere. It's tiring just thinking about it, and it's even more tiring for the person experiencing it. Trauma studies show that the survivor's energy becomes focused on suppressing inner chaos at the expense of spontaneous involvement in their life. No wonder it becomes increasingly difficult for some people to "get things done." We spend all the energy meant for our vision (not to mention the regular tasks of life) on managing our inner world.

Bottom line, survival can be both a gift and a curse. It helps us live through the tragedy, but if the effects of our trauma go undealt with, it will keep us from living out our purpose. I've learned that we can even be affected by the trauma we didn't directly experience. It could be generational trauma, trauma in utero, or collective trauma, like the effects of police brutality on the African American community. At the time of this writing, we're still experiencing the collective trauma of the COVID-19 Pandemic.

Whatever our experiences are, acute or complex, individual or communal, it all matters. It impacts how we see ourselves, how we interact with others, and how we pursue vision. If we don't have the proper tools and support, our main aim will always be self-preservation.

The Other Side of Self-Preservation

Granted, we know we are hardwired for survival, but what I'm talking about is the side of self-preservation, where we do things that undermine our efforts towards something better. Trauma is not always the cause of this. Self-preservation can simply be about preserving the sense of self we've always known or feel comfortable with.

This can result in unhealthy cycles of self-sabotage, pro-crastination, coping mechanisms, and people-pleasing. Self-sabotage is characterized by behaviors that directly work against our dreams and goals. Like wanting to lose 30 pounds but choosing late-night fast-food runs. Or, because of a strong fear of failure, we unconsciously do poorly at work, show up late, and procrastinate - all so we don't get promoted or shown new opportunities.

GAP Community founder Jean-Marie Job refers to this as **self-protection**. In her book, *The ART of Feeding Heroes: Leading from the Inside Out*, she says, *"Self-protection, in a less useful context, seduces us to play small, hold back, hide ourselves and live in scarcity."* To be fair, it's possible we aren't even aware of what we're really doing or the undesirable outcomes our actions cause.

These cycles work kind of like a thermostat in our lives. We have an unconscious perception of what we deserve, what we can handle, and where we should be in life. We do our best to make sure we maintain that position. Whenever our life is out of line with our unconscious perceptions, the thermostat kicks on. What's interesting about self-sabotage is that it actually reinforces what we're afraid of. What we perceive actually becomes our reality. Psychologists call this a self-fulfilling prophecy.

Mediocrity

When we choose to live in cycles like these, what we're really choosing is mediocrity. I once heard about a group of people who set out to climb to the top of a mountain. Halfway up the mountain sat a restaurant where people often stopped to refresh. Like so many others, the group reached the restaurant, and started to relax. They decided they didn't need to go any further and went back down. Maybe they thought *"What if we don't make it the rest of the way"* or *"What if something goes wrong?"* Either way, they chose mediocrity that day.

Interestingly enough, the etymology of the word mediocre means "halfway to the top." When it comes to success and vision, we may only allow ourselves to go so far. We might not let ourselves completely fail, but we settle for doing just enough and being average. Like I said, trauma may not have anything to do with it, but there are negative self-perceptions at play working to maintain what we believe about ourselves.

People-Pleasing

Self-preservation also looks like remaining in the boxes other people create for us. Somewhere along the way, we've embraced a label or image they placed on us. In order to keep the peace, both internally and in the relation-ship, we just go along with it. This continues even when we don't want to believe it about ourselves or keep up the act anymore.

Sometimes others don't create the box, but we create it for ourselves. We make up what we think is required to keep people in our lives happy, or to ensure that see us, praise us, they don't leave us, or whatever we need them to do to keep things the way we want it. People-pleasing in this way can even be subconscious at times because it's a way of thinking and behaving we picked up from childhood. Somewhere along the way we learned what worked for us and the people we were in close rela-tionship with, mainly our parents, and carried those same strategies into adulthood. That said, people-pleasing will often keep us from pursuing our vision because we're more concerned about maintaining the relationship than following our dreams.

The Day That Changed My Life

I catapulted through the windshield of the car.

Just thirty minutes earlier, I was sitting in a Saturday night church service with my mom, and dad who is a pas-tor. As he sat in the pulpit preparing to preach and my mother sat in a pew towards the front, my friend helped me work through a plan to sneak out and take my mother's car without permission. I wanted to be with my girlfriend, like any other teen boy, but this particular night was special because it was her birthday. I *had* to see her. I knew I'd be met with a definite "no" if I asked my mom to go, so the plan commenced. My friend and I snuck out. We drove to the nearby restaurant where some of our other friends were, and my girl met us there. After chatting for a bit, my friend took the car back, so my parents wouldn't notice it was gone. My girlfriend would drop me off at home later. I had it all worked out.

After getting in the passenger side of my girl's car and putting on the seatbelt, I quickly realized that wasn't going to work. You see, I had on this dope oversized Chicago Bulls jacket... and the seat belt was causing it to bunch up. So, in order to preserve my *swag*, I took the seat belt off, leaned my seat back, and tried to look cool. Moments later, it began to rain, causing the windshield to become blurry. As I turned to ask my girlfriend if she could turn the windshield wipers on, I catapulted through the windshield of the car and jerked back into the passenger seat.

It all happened so fast. One moment, my lips were fixed to say "turn" and the next, it felt like I wasn't even in my body anymore. I could hear my girlfriend screaming and crying, though her sound was becoming fainter by the second. At the time, I didn't feel any pain. I just remember hearing myself repeat, "Please Lord, I don't want to die. I don't want to die!"

Yes, I Survived

As soon as feeling returned to my hands and feet, I darted out of the car. Looking back, I don't know how I escaped, but when I did, I started running down the street as fast as I could. At some point, I vividly remember a man stopped me and told me to sit down on the curb. It was the strangest thing because once I sat down, I didn't feel any pain anymore. This stranger proceeded to hand me a Styrofoam cup filled with water and told me to *"drink the water, then spit out the blood."* I obliged, and he continued to give me cup after cup. *"Drink the water, spit out the blood."* *"Drink the water, spit out the blood."* I was so confused; *"Where was he getting the water and cups from,"* I thought to myself, but I just kept doing as I was told.

After the water, he asked me to tell him my name and I responded, "Jonathan." He then asked where I lived, and I gave him the address. He repeated these same questions to me again and again. I responded the same each time. Then, he told me that the police were on the way, and upon arriving, they would ask me the same questions. He warned me that answering incorrectly would make them think something was wrong with my head. He also warned me not to inform the police that he coached me on this because if I did, they would think I was crazy - maybe like you as you're reading this. At the moment, it didn't cross my mind, but in hindsight, I think that man might have been an angel sent to save my life. There was something about him and his voice that calmed me, and while in his presence, I couldn't feel any pain.

Suddenly, he said, "*the police are coming,*" and immediately, the sound of sirens pierced my ears. At once, I could feel pain register all over my body, like I had been hit by a truck. It was then that I realized how badly injured I was. There was blood everywhere, and the pain was excruciating. Once the police arrived, they began to secure my head, and indeed asked me the same questions the stranger told me to remember. They kept repeating them. Then they asked how I got out of the car and I told them that I just walked out of it. A look of shock appeared on their faces, and they proceeded to say, "*There's no way you could have gotten out of that car, sir. How did you get out of the car?*" So, I told them that I didn't know. Later, I found out we were hit by a minivan that completely totaled my girlfriend's car. It's hard to recall, but I think she was still trapped inside, and the paramedics had to rescue her. When they took me to the hospital and I gathered what was happening, I immediately begged, "*Please don't call my mom!*" I knew I was going to be in a lot of trouble.

Inside the hospital room, I remember five or six doctors

deliberating back and forth on how to proceed with treatment. They didn't know how to handle my level of trauma. So, for hours, they reached out to all the doctors in the local area and none were available. All of a sudden, someone called, and it happened to be the number one plastic surgeon in Pasadena. The doctor came to the hospital and immediately began surgery. He had to do a lot of work on my face, because the glass from the windshield punctured it so badly and caused some damage to my eye. So much so that they believed I would not see out of it again. When my mom arrived, she entered the hospital room, took one look at me, and immediately passed out.

Amazingly, I was released to go home later the same night. Yes, I survived the car accident, but the days ahead would be no easy battle. Most would agree that "surviving" the accident, the loss, the relationship, or the abuse is only the beginning. Maybe for some, it's the easiest part. It's the months and years of trying to live afterward that can be challenging. Wouldn't you agree?

Scar Management

After the accident, I didn't want to go to school because I didn't want people to see my face. Even after the scar from my surgery healed, I found myself subconsciously trying to cover it. In full transparency, the scar reiterated a perception I already had about myself that I wasn't handsome. This was a belief I carried for some time and then it was amplified as a result of my trauma. This impacted my self-image for years to come.

In an effort to manage our metaphorical scars - the things that highlight our insecurities - we hide, shrink, or don't even show up at all. Scars become significant and painful. But it shouldn't be this way. If we let them, our scars can remind that we are *overcomers*. They don't have to be the parts of us we hide or try to forget.

Misery Loves Company

In the biblical story, Joshua and Caleb were eager to enter the Promised Land. But the majority cried, complained, and even threatened to kill them. They said, "*If only we had died in Egypt! Or in this wilderness! Why is the Lord bringing us to this land only to let us fall by the sword?*" Then they said to each other, "*We should choose a leader and go back to Egypt.*" Who's to say everyone actually thought going back to Egypt was a good idea? If I had to guess, I'd say it was probably a small, loud group that influenced everyone else.

I've learned that misery really does love company. Sometimes we encounter people in life who choose to make *survival* their permanent residence. In other words, they've become so influenced by the thermostat I mentioned earlier that they've elected themselves as the thermostat for others. They influence people toward a small view of God and a small view of their purpose. They might have the best intentions to bring comfort, support, or wisdom of some kind... but this worldview ultimately harms people. It brings them to a place where they become filled with disappointment and despair. Friends don't let friends hold onto unhealthy mindsets.

For the sake of their identity, I will refer to the person in this story as "The Pusher." As I sat at home, recovering from one of the most traumatic experiences in my life, The Pusher came into my bedroom and proclaimed, *"The Lord did this to you."* This naturally caused a tragic situation to go from bad to horribly worse. Why would they say that? How could they have thought that was going to be helpful? I wonder if someone's ever said something like that to you.

In my experience, people like The Pusher hold onto the belief that we should accept life as it is. Remember, *surviving* is the number one goal, not thriving. We should accept life as it is; after all, these are the cards we've been dealt. Some go so far as to blame God for traumatic experiences. "This was His will," "He's in control," and if something bad happens, "Don't question why, just accept it." They say these things because they can't think of a reasonable explanation themselves or they don't want to deal with the actual pain of what happened.

Worst of all, the "pushers" often come in during the middle of our struggle to make sense out of it all. Our perception of the situation is currently malleable, and that's when they decide to say what they say. This ultimately causes our self-view to get muddled and leads to unfavorable life choices. After all, if God has it out for me, then I should do whatever it takes to save my own skin. Or, if pain is so inevitable, and I'm not so important, then it doesn't really matter what I do.

As the son of a preacher, I had always heard that the devil was out to get me. While I admit that preacher's kids often have a hard time growing up, that's really not a helpful thing to hear! When the Pusher told me that the Lord caused my car accident, that he wanted it to happen, my 17-year-old mind concluded that God must have been on the same team as the devil. That's two against one, and I obviously can't win.

So, I decided I would *take myself out of the equation all together.* I opened the cupboard, got a razor blade, went into the bathroom, and locked the door. As I began to apply the razor to my wrist, my mom suddenly came banging on the door, shouting, *"Boy, what are you doing in there?"* *"Uh, nothing momma, nothing,"* I responded, and she demanded that I open the door. I opened the door, and immediately, she grabbed me and held me in her arms.

From that day forward, my family decided they wouldn't allow any more "pushers" in the house.

Like I said, I don't think people's intentions are to harm us. I don't think we start out life intending to harm ourselves, either. It's just that life experiences and trauma influence our perceptions so much so that we begin to believe lies. We embrace a skewed perception of events, people, and ourselves. We let negative voices and thoughts shape us. We start to think, "This is just the way I am," or "This is just how life is for me."

Some of the Children of Israel believed wandering in the wilderness was their only option. Others thought that going back to Egypt was preferable. Maybe they thought they would never really know or experience the Promised Land. So why not just keep wandering around, or worse, go back to slavery altogether?

It's really no different for us. All we know is what has "worked" for us in the past, what has helped us survive. Even if these things keep us from our vision pursuit, we still hold onto them. My life would look very different if I still allowed the effects of my accident and the mentality of the "pusher" to shape how I live. As you process your experiences with trauma and life, see if you can identify your own cycles and the underlying beliefs. You might not like what you see, but it's the first step toward choosing something better.

TAKE A MOMENT TO

What similarities do you find between yourself and the Children of Israel?

YOUR PURPOSE IS THE SOLUTION

PROCEED WITH COURAGE

"One needs a vision of the Promised Land in order to have the strength to move."

~ Leo Tolstoy

In the last couple of chapters, we saw how perception is one of the biggest factors that hinders us on our journey to pursuing vision. Our life experiences cause us to see ourselves a certain way, trauma keeps us stuck, and the influence of others often gives us a warped perspective. We need courage if we are ever going to make it. The path ahead requires courage to do something different, to become who we were always meant to be.

Take a moment to close your eyes. Actually close your eyes and imagine yourself living in the fullness of your vision and dreams. What do you look like? What will you be doing? What kind of impact will you be making? Take a couple of minutes and dream.

What if I told you it was all possible? Though it sounds cliché, all you have to do is believe. In the next couple of chapters, I'll address some things that will help us change our limiting perceptions and actions, so that we can be free to experience the possibilities of our purpose.

For the Children of Israel, their self-perception didn't allow them to enter the Promised Land. But God didn't allow them to go back into captivity either. Everything got harder, but they kept going towards the promise anyway. T.D. Jakes said, "Run in the direction of your dream, not your disease." To be clear, I'm not referring to our issues with perception or the effects of our trauma as a disease. However, when broken down, the word becomes "dis" – "ease," meaning without comfort.

As you evaluate your life experiences and perceptions, I want to encourage you to keep running towards your vision, instead of what you're used to running to when your vision makes you uncomfortable.

PART THREE

BEYOND SEEING

CHAPTER 10
I AM NOT A GRASSHOPPER

"I Am. Two of the most powerful words; for what you put after them shapes your reality."

~ Bevan Le

Joshua and Caleb experienced slavery and journeyed in the wilderness like everyone else. They also saw the giants firsthand, yet they still wanted to pursue the Promised Land. While the others wallowed in self-pity, something within those two gave them the courage to go after their rightful inheritance. They gave a good report, but deep down, they embraced the reality of their vision and purpose. This empowered them to proceed in spite of the very real obstacles and fears. If Joshua and Caleb were modern-day protestors, I think we'd see them marching through the Israelite camp carrying signs and shouting. "I am not a grasshopper! I am not a grasshopper!"

If you don't know already, what we say about ourselves is a manifestation of what we truly believe about ourselves. *"Out of the abundance of the heart, the mouth speaks – Luke 6:45b."* Change can't just stop at our words; it has to inform our beliefs.

Another thing I heard Jean Jobs say is, *"Beliefs shift as they are questioned and explored."* If our references shape our beliefs and our perception is tied to the definitions we embrace,

> What we say about ourselves is a manifestation of what we truly believe about ourselves.

then we've found our true starting point. *To counter the Grasshopper Complex, one must learn to lay down the false perceptions previously accepted.* This means changing our references and redefining what we encounter in a way that pushes us forward.

Learn from Others

We can change our references by examining other people's stories. When we see how they overcame obstacles, hardship, and adverse life experiences, we gain a new reference for ourselves. It isn't always as easy as *"If they did it, I can too,"* but we will glean wisdom and insight from their tenacity and courage. Many successful business owners, inventors, authors, artists, and entertainers have stories we would be surprised by. They do expand what we view as possible for ourselves.

Have you ever heard of the cleaning product 409? Did you know it gained that name because the creators failed 408 times before developing what they called the "miracle cleaner"? Or that Steven Spielberg was rejected from film school three times, then later dropped out after being accepted, so he could direct a movie? What about Walt Disney? He was once fired by a newspaper editor because he "lacked imagination and had no good ideas."

One of my favorite stories is the story of Sylvester Stallone, who once said, *"Success is usually the culmination of controlling failure."* At 28, Stallone moved from New York to California with his wife. He was a struggling actor who hit desperate times trying to find work in the industry. One day, Stallone saw a story on television about a fighter that inspired him. His mother told him she felt writing may be an avenue to his success. Hearing this, he sat down and wrote a screenplay. He believed that if he could find someone to produce it, he would star as the lead actor. Sounds like wishful thinking, right? Well, after completing the screenplay, he quickly got a bite from a film producer who wanted to purchase his script. The problem was the producer wanted an acclaimed Hollywood actor to play the lead role. Stallone, with his back against the wall, made the tough decision to turn down the $100,000 offer from the producer to purchase his screenplay. The producer called Stallone again and offered even more money, but he stood his ground. Either the producer would cast Stallone as the lead actor in his own screenplay, or he couldn't purchase the script. Finally, the producer gave in, allowing Stallone to play the lead role... but only agreed to pay him $35,000 for the script and the acting. Stallone accepted the offer, and the rest is history.

The movie *Rocky* has made over $100 million at the box office and launched the career of Sylvester Stallone. In 1977, *Rocky* was nominated for ten Oscars and won three, including Best Picture. While Stallone doesn't own the *Rocky* franchise, he originated it, and he's made millions on deals for the movies. Stallone was an insignificant, inexperienced actor who took a bold stance before the Hollywood heavyweights of his day. Like Joshua and Caleb, he didn't allow anyone to force him to abandon his dream. He didn't allow his struggles to stop him. Rocky Balboa said it best, *"Every champion was once a contender who refused to give up."*

What we learn from Stallone and others is that failure, rejection, and disappointment are all a part of the journey, but they aren't meant to determine our destination. Our destination is our purpose and vision. Negative experiences are just things we experience along the way. While most would call these experiences bad, I want to offer an alternative: Consider seeing them as gifts.

I know, it doesn't really make sense. How could something like failure or rejection be a gift? Well, if we learn to redefine and ultimately respond differently, the outcome will be better for us. We can learn from every negative experience. Every failure, heartbreak, and disappointment get us closer to our cleaning product 409 moment.

I love the way Michael Jordan talks about failure. He once said, "*I've missed more than 9,000 shots in my career. I've lost almost 300 games. Twenty-six times I've been trusted to take the game winning shot and missed. I've failed over and over and over again in my life and that is why I succeed." Failure is nothing more than an opportunity for us to learn and grow, which leads to success.* Don't embrace a definition of failure that tells you that you're not capable or worthy.

The same goes for rejection and disappointment. Recently, I've taken on the perspective that it's impossible to be disappointed. Hear me out. I have experienced the unpleasant feeling that comes with unmet expectations, which by definition is disappointment. But after looking at the root of the word, which means to "deprive of position" or "reverse an appointment," I've decided disappointment isn't a possibility for me. Since vision and purpose were given to me by God, there's nothing that can reverse what I've been appointed for. The same applies to you. Don't allow rejection, failure, and unexpected outcomes to deter you from pursuing your vision. I like to think of vision as water, because when faced with an obstacle like a log in a river, water continues to flow around it.

Mentors Are a Must

You can also gain new references and learn from others by getting a mentor or two. I strongly believe in having mentors for several reasons, but first, let me just say, mentors don't have to be someone who meets with you for lunch monthly. Sometimes our mentors are found in books, YouTube videos, and through experiences like conferences and seminars. I have some mentors who I may never meet, but that doesn't take away from the value they've added to my life. Proverbs 27:17 says, "*Iron sharpens iron, and one person sharpens the wits of another.*"

If we look at the full story, we see that Joshua and Caleb probably had a positive perception due to their strong relationship with Moses. They saw how Moses led the children of Israel out of captivity and his leadership while they were in the wilderness. They also saw some of Moses' private moments and his relationship with God. As a mentor, Moses helped develop Joshua by affirming his gifts and empowering him to lead during battle. It was Joshua who eventually led the Children of Israel into the Promised Land after their sentence of wandering, which can be attributed to Moses' leadership, but also Joshua's "followership."

In a digital toolbox I developed for my organization, Session 5, I talked about "10 Steps to Finding a Good Mentor" and "17 Steps to Being an Exceptional Mentee." You need to understand both. One of the things to consider when finding a good mentor is, "Is my mentor always learning and growing in their field? Are they looking for technologies or better techniques?" Another thing to consider is, "Does my mentor have mentors?" We all need feedback, including those who mentor us. If someone wants to mentor me, they need to receive feedback from someone else and grow from it themselves.

When it comes to being an exceptional mentee, you have to show that you're serious about growing and learning. How? For one, respect your mentor's time. Come to meetings prepared with questions. Tell the truth about your current mindsets, actions, and results. Minimize distractions when you are together. Support your mentor's events. This goes especially for business and career events. When you serve your mentors, you get to learn indirectly from the way they operate, and it often opens unexpected doors.

Exposure is key for changing our references. Whether it's through a mentor, the internet, an event, or entering a whole new circle of people to learn and grow with, exposure and new experiences will begin to shape how we see ourselves and pursue vision.

Use Your Superpowers

Another way to change our references and redefine our reality is called *reframing*. We frequently get accustomed to focusing on one aspect of the picture in our lives. It's like putting an 11x14 photo in a 5x7 frame. You'll only see certain details while missing others. One psychologist noted, *"There are many other experiences you could have chosen. Which stories you choose communicates the frame within which you view your life."* Is there more to the story? Are there details in the picture of your life that could serve you better than the ones you currently live by?

We all have internal superpowers we can use to shift our perception or reframe our experiences; I made reference to one of them in the Vision Continuum. I want to focus on the power of words, the power of intake, the power of projection, and the power of pain and pleasure. We can categorize them as **The Four P's**.

The power of words is significant, possibly more than we realize. That's why language and understanding the meaning of words is so important to me. Consider this quote by author Betty Eadie, *"If we understood the power of our thoughts, we would guard them more closely. If we understood the awesome power of our words, we would prefer silence to almost anything negative. In our thoughts and words, we create our own weaknesses and our own strengths."* Similarly, Proverbs 18:21 says, *"Life and death are in the power of the tongue."* What we say to and about ourselves shapes our beliefs, which shape our actions, and so on. We can use this power positively through affirmations.

Muhammad Ali said, *"It's the repetition of affirmations that leads to belief. Once that belief becomes a deep conviction, things begin to happen."* Ali is most known for his declaration, *"I am the greatest,"* and he was. Hal Elrod, author and success coach, said, *"Your self-talk has dramatic influence on your level of success in every aspect of your life... your affirmations are typically working for or against you depending on how you are using them."* If you take time to evaluate your internal conversation, what would you observe?

Next is the power of intake. Just like what we say, we need to manage what we see and hear. Have you ever thought about why our eyes, mouth, and ears are all connected to our heads? It's because they are indirectly connected to our brains. What we take in matters greatly. Thus, the power of intake is the conscientious ability to monitor and assess what one allows to penetrate and influence one's mind, emotions, perceptions, and values.

If you recall, I mentioned earlier about how much money is spent on advertising. The things we look at and listen to constantly shape us, whether it's music, social media, movies, the news, or advertisements. We'll take on the references, many negative, if we don't take a step back and consider our intake. Doing something like a 30-day media fast is a great way to do a negative reference detox. However, when you do something like this, it's important to *replace it* with something positive, like listening to motivational podcasts, reading books, or watching inspirational videos on YouTube.

The better the ideas we expose ourselves to, the more we'll be able to benefit from the power of projection. This is where imagination comes into the picture. We have the ability to place our minds in a space where our physical bodies have not yet arrived. This is similar to the practice of visualization, which is becoming more widely known and used. Celebrities, athletes, and other highly successful individuals often share about its significant role in their own personal success.

As Hal Elrod explains in his book *The Miracle Morning*, *"Visualization, also known as creative visualization or mental rehearsal, refers to the practice of seeking to generate positive results in your outer world by using your imagination to create mental pictures of specific behaviors and outcomes occurring in your life."* When it comes to pursuing vision, using the power of projection can help us stay motivated and inspired.

There's also the power of pain and pleasure. I've already talked about how my traumatic, painful, near-death experience and the response from the pusher affected my self-perception. Pleasure can also impact our perception of ourselves, for better or for worse. Chasing it can keep us from seeing things as they really are, or even dull our perceptions. We have to remember that while our experiences are real, and our emotions about them are legitimate, we don't have to let them inform our entire self-view.

Look in the Mirror

The truth of the matter is, sometimes we don't have to go very far to get new references. We just have to learn to look in the mirror and embrace the person we see looking back at us, without any judgment. I know we've been talking about perception this whole time, but who you really are, what you're gifted at, and what you've accomplished doesn't change simply because you have a hard time seeing it.

Your natural gifts, talents, and abilities can serve as a reference for you to use. Sometimes, we disregard our natural gifts because we don't think they have meaning. The reality is, they do. There's a reason you're attracted to certain hobbies, jobs, types of people, etc. If you take time to look in the mirror and assess your life, you may find some inspiration and motivation. You may recognize that you're not simply what you've experienced or what you feel about yourself.

TAKE A MOMENT TO

What are some beliefs or actions you currently have that you need new references for?

CHAPTER 11
THE GOAL ISN'T BETTER

"Intentionality pulls you to greatness"

~ Evan Money

At the end of the day, we want more than simply getting better. "Better" is an adjective that describes something "of a more excellent or effective type or quality." That means something can go from horrible to bad and by definition get "better." Even when we get a bit better, we're still just one step away from going back to who we were. I believe when we make better our aim, we really just set ourselves up to make changes we feel comfortable with. We determine a measure of progress without feedback and settle for less.

On the other hand, pursuing vision requires us to *transform*. Remember, it's like a chisel. It sculpts us into something completely different from where we started.

If we allow it, vision transforms us into the fullness of who we were always meant to be, not just settling for some better version of who we were. I'm not saying better isn't good, it just shouldn't be our goal. Instead, we should focus on our vision pursuit and become the best version of ourselves.

Be Your Own Hero

In her book, "*The Art of Feeding Heroes,*" Jean Jobs says, "*I have learned that every transformation in someone's life is an exchange. It is an exchange between the status quo and a new possibility, between settling and stretching... between death and life. It is watching someone who has never felt validated or good enough decide to finally stand and speak up, to use his or her voice in a moment of transformation. It is a heroic act.*"

She goes on to say, "*Transformation is violent, it is more than insight - insight only gives the illusion of transformation.*" That is to say, reading this book and others like it isn't enough. You could add podcasts, seminars, and conferences to the mix, and you still only get insight. You have to choose to make changes along with the knowledge you acquire. If you don't, you'll always find yourself hindered by your perceptions, issues with capacity, and lack of true accountability.

One of my mentors talks about the constant intake of information with no change in action. They say it puts us in a "doom loop." We grow in self-awareness and get so caught up in the theory of "getting better" that we just stay in a loop. This actually leads to self-destruction and not self-improvement. All the "I shoulds" – "I should be doing," "I should know," "I should have," and so on create debilitating pressure... or what my mentor calls "doom." Let me know if you've ever felt that way. So, what do we do to avoid the doom loops?

We have to take deliberate, practical steps towards transformation. Transformation is intentional, not magical. Over the years, the culmination of our life experiences gives us a way of thinking, acting, and relating to others. We get accustomed to the habits and shortcuts that have helped us in the past. Rewiring all this takes effort. No one just wakes up and eliminates all the things negatively impacting their life in

> Transformation is intentional, not magical.

a single day. We have to be intentional and committed, especially if we're serious about our vision. Don't wait for someone to rescue you from yourself. Be your own hero by taking active steps toward change.

Transformation Starts in the Mind

You've probably gathered that this whole book is about transforming your mind, in a sense. Perception boils down to what we believe. The Grasshopper Mentality comes from deeply held beliefs. If our beliefs are what hinders us, then they must be changed. The Apostle Paul said, *"Be transformed by the renewing of your mind."* George Bernard Shaw puts it this way, *"Those who can't change their minds, can't change anything."* How intentional are you when it comes to your thinking? Do you actually process your thoughts throughout the day?

Research shows that on any given day, the average person thinks somewhere between 50,000 and 60,000 thoughts. Hal Elrod says, *"The problem is that ninety-five percent of our thoughts are the same as the ones we thought the day before."* Like we talked about with the power of intake, if we don't take time to assess our thoughts and insert new ones, our lives will continue to be shaped by how we have always thought. This will lead us to mediocrity.

One day, I was baking cookies with a friend. I prepped the dough, grabbed the cookie sheet, and proceeded to place aluminum foil over it. My friend stopped me and asked, *"Why are you putting foil on the sheet?"* *"Well, that's what my mom always did,"* I responded. He proceeded to tell me it was a nonstick pan. I realized that I never thought about *why* I always placed the foil down. I just did what I had always done.

Our unexamined thoughts often lead to unexamined actions. While putting foil on a nonstick cookie sheet isn't that big of a deal, it indicates a deeper problem. We all have habits that inadvertently work against our goals. We all lack habits that would propel us toward our vision. Be honest with yourself.

> Our unexamined thoughts often lead to unexamined actions

It's in the Day to Day

Vision, or what I call your overall vision, will directly impact what I call your **life vision**. Your life vision is the day-to-day things you need to do to become what you've identified as your overall vision. It's like the engine driving you toward your destination.

For example, let's say someone's overall vision is to become the best basketball player in the league. What do they have to do to accomplish this? Establish healthy eating habits, create a practice routine, and so on. It's the same with us in our pursuit of vision. I recall John Maxwell saying something along the lines of, "*Most people have a plan for everything else, but growing.*" We make plans to lose weight, obtain degrees and certifications, spend less on the credit card, etc. These are all great, but they aren't a real plan for our overall vision. We need a plan that goes down to the level of our real habits and routines. This is directly tied to building capacity.

When I was praying about my own personal life and a much-needed routine, I developed **70/30**. It's 70 minutes of activity in the morning and 30 minutes of activity in the evening, 100 minutes dedicated to growth every day. Feel free to try it out for yourself. It's important for me to emphasize that it's not really about the time, but *what you do with the time* and how each item ultimately benefits your vision. Here's what it looks like for me:

Morning: 70 Minutes

10 Minutes | Exercise:

Exercise is so essential for a number of reasons. Vision has to work through your body. If you're healthy and taking care of your body to ensure optimal health, you'll have an easier time accomplishing your vision. A lack of health, on the other hand, complicates and hinders us.

10 minutes is not a long time. You could take a morning walk or run or do some quick cardio or yoga in your house. The goal is to get up and get your body moving. Surprisingly, exercising in the morning actually helps you

rest better later, along with a number of other great benefits. When I started this routine, I instantly began to feel more energized and clearer in my thinking.

15 Minutes | Prayer/ Meditation:

Prayer or meditation is important for our mental and emotional care. Of course, more time can be dedicated to it, but 15 minutes is far better than zero. During this time, I focus on three primary things:

1. Addressing all of my negative feelings, concerns, worries, and anxieties. I do this first. If I allow myself, I will spend the whole "morning 70" in a negative headspace, and it will affect my emotions for the rest of the time, potentially for the rest of the day.

2. I spend the next 5 minutes being grateful. Sometimes I have to force myself to do this. I think about all the things I have to be grateful for and look forward to in the day.

3. I spend the last five minutes in silence. I call this a time of impartation where I quiet myself so that I can hear from God. In meditation, this is where you open your mind to creative thoughts, or simply let whatever comes to your mind come.

10 Minutes | Read or Say Your Vision Out loud:

When we speak out loud to ourselves, we internalize our words. This is a great way to embrace our vision. Research shows that speaking out loud engages our brains differently than when we are simply thinking to ourselves. It powerfully impacts our confidence and self-esteem. When you do this, you should use the same energy and excitement that would be generated as if what you're saying is your current reality. Every day, I quote the following:

> "I, Jonathan DeCuir, am one of the most sought-after voices that God uses to proclaim wholeness as His central theme – while encouraging people toward their Kingdom purpose... I will faithfully execute the brilliant strategies I have received and courageously overcome every single challenge until my goal has been achieved... I am charging my entire being to be fully focused, consistently self-disciplined, and to have a maximizing mindset."

I can't even begin to tell you the impact it has had on my life and my approach to my vision. When I started, I would read it from a paper, then I recorded myself and would listen to it and repeat it; now I have it memorized. It's now a part of me, but did you catch how it started? *I read it from a piece of paper.* If we want to habitualize reading our vision aloud, we have to write it down first. The prophet Habakkuk said, *"Write the vision and make it plain."*

10 Minutes | Visualization:

Once you've spoken your vision out loud, it's time to visualize. This is where the power of projection and working your imagination muscle comes into play. Visualization is becoming more widely known and used as celebrities, athletes, and other highly successful individuals share about its significant role in their own personal success. There's an article that explains, *"When athletes imagine perfect performance often enough, neural pathways become conditioned to actually achieve what they imagined."* As mentioned before, Hal Elrod notes, *"Visualization, also known as creative visualization or mental rehearsal, refers to the practice of seeking to generate positive results in your outer world by using your imagination to create mental pictures of specific behaviors and outcomes occurring in your life."* Take time to use your imagination, picturing yourself being and doing what you desire.

When I think about my vision, I visualize myself in a venue full of people, some in-person and some virtual, but I can see them all. I am on the stage. I can see how I look and what I am wearing. I visualize myself being introduced, walking out, and delivering a powerful message or motivational talk. I can see people's reactions, how they're being impacted, and so on. I'm not painting a picture, but I'm creating a cinematic experience of sorts that I'll one day live.

This practice may seem unconventional... but it's a muscle most of us already use. In some circles, the use of our imagination is combined with what we call faith. Seeing and believing what doesn't yet exist. It's also something people use when they worry and imagine worst-case scenarios. We worry so much, but rather than worrying, let's use our imagination for something that actually serves us.

15 Minutes | Reading:

This is connected to learning and can happen through other media, but there's something especially beneficial about the act of reading. Reading develops the mind, strengthens the brain, builds vocabulary, reduces stress, and the list goes on. My mentor Evan said, *"The way you get to the next level is by standing on the books you read."* Reading exposes us to new information, catapulting us toward our vision. It also helps us change and improve our references, which ultimately helps us reach our dreams. If you're not an avid reader, you'd be surprised at how many books you will read if you commit to just 15 minutes a day.

10 Minutes | Learning:

Last comes the ten minutes of learning. This is a little different from the reading session because this can be done by watching videos, engaging in an online course, or exploring new resources that will help you with your vision. This could be learning from someone who is doing what you want to do, learning about what you want to do, or about something that will help you accomplish your vision better. You know the common saying, *"Work smarter, not harder."* An example of this could be learning about project management tools and software, watching TED Talks, or taking a course on a platform like Udemy or the Session 5 Institute *(shameless plug)*.

Evening: 30 Minutes

10 Minutes | Reflective Gratitude:

Take some time to reflect on your day. What good things happened? What did you experience? What are you grateful for? Do you have anything to look forward to tomorrow? I love what Zig Ziglar says about gratitude: *"Gratitude is the healthiest of all human emotions. The more you express gratitude for what you have, the more likely you will have even more to express gratitude for."* Additionally, the Greek storyteller Aesop once said, *"Gratitude turns what we have into enough."* It may be useful to have a prayer or gratitude journal where you can write out your prayers and what you're grateful for so that you can go back and review it when you need encouragement.

10 Minutes | Prepare for the Next Day:

Take some time to review your calendar and think about how you want each event to go. What do you want to accomplish? How do you want to show up at meetings or events? What are you going to wear? Do you need to prep breakfast and lunch ahead of time? Some people set the timer on their coffee machines, so that coffee can be brewing in the morning. Do whatever you need to do that would be most helpful for your next day.

10 Minutes| Read Your Vision Out Loud (Again):

How you end your night impacts how you begin your next day. That's why the evening routine is so important. I want the last thing I think about each night to be the overall vision God has given me. I want it to influence how I dream, and all the subconscious processes that occur when I sleep. Imagine how differently your day might go after a nightly routine like this.

You may find yourself spending more or less time than my proposed 70/30. That's okay. Remember, the goal is to commit to a routine and engage in activities that positively impact your vision. The purpose of the plan, whether you choose to incorporate 70/30 in your life or something else, is to keep you growing. Let positive habits transform you. Speaking of which...

Let's Talk Habits

I recently read a book called *The Power of Habits* by Charles Duhigg. I won't go too deep into habits, but to be clear, habits differ from routines. While habits may be considered a type of routine or a part of your routine, they function a bit differently. You have to be intentional about routines, whereas habits are learned, repeated behaviors that become automatic and sometimes unconscious.

As explained in the book, habits are a loop that consists of a cue or trigger, a response, and a reward. If we understand how habits work, then we can change them. Like Duhigg said, *"Most of our intensely ingrained beliefs and routines are just simple habit loops. They are what we are used to, but they are not us. They are not who we are at our core. We can change them!"*

A habit's cue can be connected to time, place, presence of people, a particular emotion, or a behavior that has become ritualized. For instance, when it hits midnight, I find myself automatically thinking about going to

In-N-Out. Another common example is nail-biting. People who bite their nails are typically cued by an emotion like stress, anxiety, or boredom. Some say that all habits are neurologically motivated by a need to relieve pain or discomfort. Even though it can cause some physical pain, a habit like nail-biting gives the reward of relieving mental tension. Habits are perpetuated by the rewards we receive from performing an action.

So, changing your habits requires self-awareness and self-management. You have to think about your responses to everyday stimuli. What do you do when you first open your eyes? What do you do when you feel stressed and overwhelmed? What do you do when you feel lonely or afraid? Once you become aware of your trigger and your automatic response, you can work towards changing your habit. Make sure your new habit produces a good reward, though!

The Power of Habits also mentions keystone habits, defined as *"A positive or negative habit will inform every other habit in your life."* They cascade in a domino effect. For instance, if you make a habit of changing into your workout clothes right after brushing your teeth, it could lead you into your habit of morning exercise. What's important is starting somewhere, starting small, and celebrating your wins.

It's Not One-Size-Fits-All

While understanding habits and routines are crucial, you should know it's not a one-size-fits-all kind of thing. We each have our own experiences and internal issues to address. We have to figure out which habits and routines will work best for us right now. Later on, we might need something different.

When I work with my vision coaching clients, I offer personalized solutions for them to implement in their routine. I give them custom exercises to help address issues they have. For instance, for clients who tend to work really hard and don't give themselves space to slow down, I suggest habits of rest, like taking time to recharge and be rejuvenated. I once recommended that one of my clients take 10 minutes in between meetings and activities to pray or meditate. I also encouraged them to schedule a sabbath, in other words, a day each week when they unplug and unwind. For another client who tends to focus too much on helping others, I encouraged them to develop some self-care habits, like going on a staycation and going to counseling.

When it comes to transformation, I've also come to realize we may need more unorthodox methods. For example, writing out our obituary and revisiting it every once in a while. I know this might seem a bit drastic to some, but I've found that it helps bring perspective and keep us focused, especially if we're the complacent or easily distracted type.

Another thing I've done is tell someone to have a dove release ceremony with their family and friends. The release of the doves represented the release of the "old them" to make room for who they want to become. Sometimes, we need a physical act to represent our inner commitments.

To sum up, transformation is in the day-to-day, but it may need to be jumpstarted by something unconventional. Transformation must also be maintained through personal discipline.

If you recall, from the beginning of this chapter, we saw that "transformation is violent." We'll be tempted to settle for just getting better because of what our transformation requires. But if we stay committed to the process and our vision, then our lives and those connected to us will benefit greatly. People you see operating in their greatness and living out their vision are not superhuman, magical beings. They simply brought commitment and intentionality to the mundane, day after day. Singer-songwriter David Byrne says, *"Life tends to be an accumulation of a lot of mundane decisions, which often get ignored."* It's time to pay attention and live with intention.

TAKE A MOMENT TO

Take some time to reflect on the 5 key areas of your life, (physical, financial, spiritual, emotional, and mental). Where do you see a need for transformation in each area?

What are some habits you could implement or re-implement in your life to support that transformation?

CHAPTER 12
THERE'S MORE TO THE STORY

"The way we tell our life story is the way we begin to live our life."

~ Maureen Murdock

When we look at our life and progress toward our vision and goals, we often examine all the outward behaviors. We evaluate whether they benefit us or not. Sometimes we blame others for a lack of progress. I wonder if Joshua and Caleb ever considered how and where they acted out of the Grasshopper Complex. Yes, they were ultimately the two who believed the Children of Israel could enter the Promised Land and led them there, but they must have had moments of doubt, especially when the majority went against them. How did they *really* feel when they first saw the giants? There has to be more to the story. There was definitely more to my story than I was letting on:

For the longest time, I let blame shifting and the Grasshopper Complex affect the way I felt about my dad. Don't get me wrong: He was great, and I'll cherish the relationship we had forever. But when I was younger, there were just things he did that I didn't like. I let this affect me to the point where whenever I talked about my obstacles or life challenges, I'd talk about how my relationship with my dad negatively influenced me. But there was a lot going on under the surface that I hadn't really examined, until recently.

I'm part of a men's mastermind, a small group of growth-minded men who meet quarterly. During a recent meeting, the topic of forgiveness came up. My dad came to mind immediately. But as I thought about it more deeply, I realized that I didn't really have anything to forgive him for. He hadn't really done anything wrong. So, I decided to search within and see if there was someone else I needed to forgive. Then, my mom, my self-proclaimed hero, came to mind. I suddenly realized there's a part of her story I haven't told you yet, something that affected me deeply.

My mom was rushed to the hospital and when we arrived, they told us that her aorta had split. She needed an emergency surgery, one with a low survival rate. She made it through the surgery, but the journey ahead for my sister and I was just beginning. We sacrificed a ton to journey with our mom through nine months of care. We prayed and prayed, and believed she'd be able to come home. And she did!

One day, while I was taking my mom to an outpatient facility, she said, "*Take me to Bill's Chicken.*" Despite being a Pasadena staple and one of her favorites, my reply was, "*No, I'm not taking you to Bill's Chicken.*" It wasn't the healthiest choice for my mom at the time. We went back and forth about the issue a couple of times until she yelled, "*Take me to Bill's chicken, I'm going to die anyway!*"

At that moment, something inside me shifted. I detached emotionally and mentally because I didn't want to be a part of watching my mother give up, at least, that's the story I told myself. I had always told the story of my mom being my hero. She was "Mama D." She could do anything and was there for everybody. But I kept the part of the story where I felt like she gave up a secret. I also omitted the part where I detached myself from the responsibility and opportunity to care for and be present with her - and the part of the story where I left my sister to carry the full weight of caring for our mother in her final years. That left me with a lot to process during the mastermind meeting.

I share this because I realized something: We choose to live in a portion of a story while withholding other parts of it. But the parts of the story that we hold back end up holding *us* back. If we want authentic transformation, it starts with authenticity from us. We can't hold back the dirty details anymore. We have to go through it and process it with others.

I believe that reaching our vision depends on letting go of the weight of unforgiveness. That day in the mastermind session, I realized I needed to forgive my mom for the story I had about her giving up. I also realized there was more to the story. I needed to ask forgiveness from my sister for abdicating my responsibility. Then, I needed to forgive *myself* for detaching.

> Reaching our vision depends on letting go of the weight of unforgiveness.

My mom has been gone for over 11 years, and I feel much lighter. Since the mastermind and forgiving her, the return has already proven to be exponential. Much like Return on Investment, or ROI, I have been experiencing what my mentor Evan coined as ROF, "Return on Forgiveness." My counselor Dr. Dani also said, *"Forgiveness is a thing, not everything."* Meaning forgiveness doesn't take away the reality of what happened. It doesn't always mitigate the pain, or the emotional response, but it is a step forward. The first step was allowing the other parts of the story to come to light.

Find a Release Point

As a part of our session on forgiveness during the mastermind, we were tasked to write a letter to the person we needed to forgive. As emotional as it was to write it, I did. Afterward, I was given the choice to go to the cemetery and read the letter aloud to my mom. This tangible act served as what I call a "release point" for the forgiveness that had taken place in my heart.

Release points could also look like burning a letter or item in a fire, tying something significant to balloons and watching them float away, or physically releasing doves or butterflies. The possibilities are endless, and the point is to find something you can do to represent and mark this point of release in your life. We have to process the ugly parts of the story, and we have to learn how to release things.

Do You Feel Boxed In?

As we talk about the stories of our lives, I wonder if you've ever experienced opposition from your friends and family while pursuing your vision. What story did you make up about that? "They don't want to see me grow, change, or better myself," "I feel trapped," or maybe something like "If I change, I'll lose the relationship." I've learned that people may take issue with our transformation when it begins. They aren't always ready to accept who we're becoming. They aren't comfortable when the relational or family dynamics change. So, like the thermostat I mentioned earlier, we feel tempted to go back to living in the box they've created for us. We feel the strong urge to go back to the old status quo. But we can't afford to stay in that box anymore.

Consider the story of Cinderella. I once preached a message about this, titling it "Cinderella Haters." Cinderella had a dream beyond just serving her stepmothers and sisters... but they put her into a metaphorical box. In their world, she was only good for serving them. Have you ever felt the same, with people treating you like you're only good enough to serve them and their vision, but not anything of your own? When it came down to the magical moment with the glass slipper, her family was stunned because they only saw Cinderella in the box they created for her. The question I'm sure many have pondered is, "Why didn't Cinderella just leave?"

The same happened with David in the Bible. David was a young shepherd boy who spent most of his time in the field with sheep. One day, the prophet Samuel went to David's family home and spoke to his father, Jesse. The prophet was on a hunt for the next king of Israel, and God had led him to Jesse's house. Even though David was the one God had chosen, Jesse and Samuel overlooked him. His dad didn't even invite him to the meeting with Samuel! David's family never thought it could be him. They didn't see the mighty warrior in David, or his potential to become one of the greatest kings in biblical history.

David and Cinderella both show us the idea of boxes. We all sit in boxes assigned by the perceptions of people close to us. Staying in them means passing up the opportunity to become who we were meant to be. But the boxes are usually safe and comfortable. They come from a place of familiarity and the desire to keep the status quo. Cinderella and David had family who placed them in boxes because they failed to see their real purpose. And the boxes always served the family, not David or Cinderella. We all have the choice to process the boxes we've been placed into and decide whether we want to stay or leave. Don't let people think they know you better than you know yourself, or that they have the power to dictate your life journey.

People also place us in boxes due to our mistakes and shortcomings. They tie our identity to things we did wrong. In their eyes, there's no possibility that we could become anything else. So, when we change up our act and pursue our vision, it shocks them. They assume we're following some ulterior motive. Maybe you've felt this way before.

At a deeper level, the last reason people box us in comes from our *own* self-perception and perceived inability. Remember, the Children of Israel said, *"We saw ourselves as grasshoppers in our own eyes, and we looked the same to them – Numbers 13:33."* They probably did seem small in the eyes of the people inhabiting their land, who were likened to giants, but were they really as small as grasshoppers? Sometimes the picture we show of ourselves is all people have to work with. In this case, we make the box ourselves and practically beg other people to put us in it.

On some level, this is the part of the story we don't tell. We are quick to talk about being boxed in by others, but we don't address why we choose to stay in. Let's be honest, there's a part of the box that we like. It's easier to live within the stories other people have about us. They maintain the status quo. They're familiar. When we stay in them, we keep the peace in our relationships, like we mentioned earlier. The boxes might have helped solve a problem in the past, or helped us through a trauma, but now they no longer serve us. We have to make adjustments.

In one of my graduate program classes, I was required to attend a Co-Dependents Anonymous meeting. It was so eye-opening and freeing that I kept going to several sessions beyond the minimum requirement. In the sessions, I came to terms with the boxes I had been living in.

Most of them were created for me by others, but I created some myself and I chose to stay in them.

I have counseled a number of people over the years and have heard countless stories about why people feel like they can't pursue vision because of *other people* in their life. Someone once told me that they didn't want to pursue their dreams because they feared losing relationships. They thought their success would drive people away, so they picked relationships over purpose for fear of being alone. That's a valid concern, but I wonder whether the cost is worth it in the end.

Another common thing I hear, typically from older people or parents, is they don't have time, it's too late, or, I have to wait until my children are older... which turns into it's too late. I've learned that people look for the "right time" to pursue a vision because of how they think it will impact their present roles and responsibilities. The secret is, it will never feel like a convenient time to pursue your vision. It will always require sacrifice.

Jim Carey once said, *"The decisions we make in this moment are based in either love or fear. Many choose a path out of fear disguised as practicality. What we really want seems impossibly out of reach and ridiculous to expect."* So, instead of choosing our vision, we choose what we feel makes the most sense for our life now. You'll hear no judgment from me, because sometimes, that's what we have to do for a season. But how long will we use others as an excuse for why we can't move forward?

As I continued to pursue my vision in my adulthood, I felt tension between the Jon in the box, and the Jon I wanted to become. This tension often manifested in my relationships as I transformed. When you want to get out of the boxes, you have to brace yourself for the possibility of losing people you love. You have to learn how to survive with less appreciation and validation, at least as long as it takes to form new bonds with like-minded people. This move also requires letting go of comfort, safety, and familiarity. But nothing will leave you feeling freer.

Redefine your Relationships

In today's "cancel culture" society, people are so quick to cut relationships off. Even before the onset of cancel culture, I used to believe and even preach the value of letting people go. After all, that's what you have to do to make it to the top. Now, let me just say that I think there are times when "cutting people off" or ending a relationship is necessary and healthy. This is especially true if your safety or wellbeing is in danger. But that's an entirely different category than what I'm about to explain.

After attending a personal development session, my old mindset about letting go of relationships was challenged, so I want to challenge you too. Maybe we don't need to let go of relationships that we think no longer serve us. Perhaps we need to *redefine our relationship with relationships*. Yes, you read that correctly. Our relationship with relationships has to change. What I mean is that we've grown accustomed to relating to people a certain way and when this gets disrupted, it feels like our only option is to cut the person out of our lives. But there's another way. We can step out of our boxes, so we can grow, and still maintain relationships. It requires giving the people who will object to it the time and space to accept our changes. It requires making the decision to stay connected, even if that connection looks different for a time. Someone shared with me the revelation that "*Jesus always increased His ability to make room for people no matter where they were, without it compromising who He was and where He was going.*" We can do the same thing with a little bit of patience and courage.

> Our relationship with relationships has to change.

If you wait for other people to make the necessary changes in your relationships to promote growth, nothing will ever change. Consider this statement, "*Freedom comes from taking responsibility; bondage comes from giving it away.*" Expecting others to change, to make our lives better and easier, causes us to become bound by their actions. You must take responsibility for yourself and your transformation to pursue your vision. This may mean becoming temporarily distanced or losing a relationship. However, you can still choose to make room for people in your life as long as it is within your control.

Boundaries are an Option

When I decided to redefine my relationships for the benefit of my vision pursuit, I had meetings with some of my closest friends, family, and colleagues. I knew I needed to step out of the boxes and change the stories I had been living in. But I was terrified of what they would think. I called people and explained that there was more to the story of Jon. I explained that I felt empowered to choose something different. Not everyone understood, but I felt love and support from those conversations. More importantly, I felt free. And of course, I had to deal with some people who weren't ready to accept the new Jon.

You'll need to set boundaries as you learn to redefine your relationships. The word "boundaries" typically conjures up an image of restriction, but I've come to think of them as guardrails or fences. They allow someone to move freely because they know the perimeters. In the book *Boundaries*, Dr. Henry Cloud says, *"Boundaries are simply understanding where I end, and another person begins."* Again, boundaries aren't necessarily about cutting people off, but really about making room for you to be your full self without allowing your growth to be stunted by others. Try setting small boundaries for yourself and others. It will pay off.

This could look like using the "Do Not Disturb" button while you're working. It could mean setting working hours for your vision when your family and friends know that you'll be unavailable. It could also look like not taking calls before or after a certain hour so you can get proper sleep or have time to pray and meditate in the morning. If you continue to be the go-to person who always responds, it will hold you back. You have to figure out some boundaries. Maybe you take the call but say, "I only have a few minutes right now," or "Can we talk about it a little later?" The boundaries you set in place may not always feel pleasant to you or others, but you free yourself up to grow, and extend that opportunity to others, too.

At the end of the day, *you're the only person you can control.* That makes you responsible for the vision you've received. Interestingly enough, when I looked up the etymology of "responsibility," I discovered it means to *return to the promise* that I made to myself and be accountable for it. I can't spend all my time and energy being responsible for others. I can't always choose them over myself while waiting for the right time. To help others down the line, I have to become a better version of myself first.

Let's recall the quote from Maureen Murdock at the beginning of this chapter, *"The way we tell our life story is the way we begin to live our life."* We have to be willing to tell the whole story, not just the parts that we like or don't like. We can't just tell the parts where others are the villains. More often than not, there's more to the story. When others wronged us, discounted us, and disregarded our needs, the pain was real. But if we look deeper, we'll find plenty of ways we contributed, where we also are responsible. And that's the key: Responsibility. When we decide to take responsibility for the entirety of our lives, we experience the freedom we need to pursue our vision.

TAKE A MOMENT TO

What is a story you have about yourself, your experiences, or relationships that has defined you and kept you "boxed in"?

Where in your life do you need to insert boundaries?

CHAPTER 13
FULL CIRCLE

"In their hearts human beings plan their lives, but the Lord decides where their steps will take them."

~ Proverbs 16:9

The children of Israel finally entered the Promised Land after wandering for so long. They were now able to enjoy its greatness. Perhaps everything they learned and experienced in the wilderness grew them up and caused them not to hesitate the second time. Maybe it was the leadership of Joshua and Caleb who modeled responsibility and pursuit of vision.

I believe vision is really all about the journey more than the destination. The journey equips us. All the ups, downs, frustration,

> Vision is really all about the journey more than the destination.

pain, joy, and everything else chisel us into who we are. If you take away our experiences, we wouldn't be the same person. And if we learn to embrace and respect the journey, we'll come to appreciate that it all matters for something. I'm sure that for Joshua and Caleb - the only ones who got to experience Egypt, the wilderness, AND the Promised Land - everything tasted much sweeter.

I've come to recognize that there has to be a space outside ourselves where we can be fully human and honest about our experiences. Mentors, families, and accountability groups help, but they don't go far enough. We need another space. For me, that space is God. It is where I become aware of my limiting beliefs and wrestle with perception. It's where I face the reality of my capacity, and my need for accountability. I also go to God for rest, reassurance, inspiration, direction, and healing. That's why God is my first stop on the Vision Continuum, and really where I find myself constantly returning to. Maybe the space where you experience these things isn't God, or maybe you feel like you don't have a space like this at all. I could imagine someone getting all the way to this point in the book and being disappointed or instantly turned off, but if you remember from the very beginning, I encouraged you to stay open. There's a space available for us all to process our life experiences, be human, and receive the strength, motivation, and fortitude required for our journey. I believe wherever you find yourself with God, believing or not, frustrated, skeptical, distant, or near, He's big enough to handle all of it.

No matter what, I think we can agree that we need something to help us manage the full range of emotions and experiences of life. It's a lot to process. I hope you can cultivate and engage in a space of your own, whatever it looks like. Motivational speaker Matthew Kelly said, *"We don't bear fruit by being more active, we bear more fruit by being connected to the source."* Sometimes, reaching our vision doesn't require external work. Sometimes, it takes an intentional connection to the One that created us and gave us the vision to begin with. From there, we address our issues with perception, and see our true level of capacity, and our need for accountability. Like we stated in the beginning, our vision will constantly make us evaluate these four things on the vision continuum. As we reflect, process, and take time to notice, we will soon realize that it all comes full circle. That's why it's a continuum and not a straight line.

Nothing to Lose

I was drawn to this story about Meryl Streep. In 1975, she entered an unexpected season of life that could be noted as one of the most devastating times she ever endured. Her fiancé, John Cazalea, was a very promising actor at the beginning of his movie career... but he found out he had lung cancer. Despite Meryl keeping a faithful vigil by his side, and no doubt praying for him to have the opportunity to fully realize his dreams, he succumbed to his illness. Like any couple, they wanted to enjoy the fruits of their labor and allow their love to blossom into a family.

In an article, Meryl said something I thought was interesting. When asked what part religion played in her life, she responded,

> "I follow no doctrine. I don't belong to a church or a temple or a synagogue or an ashram... So, I've always been really, deeply interested because I think I can understand the solace that's available in the whole construct of religion. But I really don't believe in the power of prayer, or things would have been avoided that have happened that are awful. So, it's a horrible position as an intelligent, emotional, yearning human being to sit outside of the available comfort there. But I just can't go there."

Meryl had barriers that stopped her from entering a spiritual space, even though she recognized it could be beneficial. I think we often run into the same problem. What hinders us from connecting to God and going deeper within? I get that this can be an uncomfortable space, but that's what we do anyway, right? We just move past the subject or altogether avoid the very thing we might need to deal with.

I'll admit it, even though I grew up in the church, was the son of a pastor, and became a pastor myself, I haven't always wanted God. I remember plenty of times when being with God was completely undesirable. It still happens from time to time. Maybe you've been there, too. Again, it may not be God, but perhaps you have trouble being still within. Sometimes, it's hard to be in "the space" when we're in a different space, like depressed, angry, disappointed, overwhelmed, sad, or even disengaged from life completely.

Shame and guilt may be at play because of something we did or didn't do. Sometimes I feel this way when I fall out of my healthy habits and routines. I don't want to go back to "God" or a healthy, spiritual space because it would be hard to get started again... plus I feel ashamed. It's like when someone goes on a diet, but they eat that one burger or dessert. Then the shame keeps them choosing unhealthy options instead of picking the diet back up.

All that to say, if you're already in a negative headspace, what do you really have to lose from being in a space that might benefit you? Even if we take God out of the equation entirely, science, success experts, and common sense list several benefits to any kind of contemplative practice. It could be mindfulness, yoga, gratitude journaling, you name it. Going to "the space" on a consistent basis only helps.

When I decide to engage in "the space," I receive exactly what I need in that moment. Sometimes it's rest, sometimes it's inspiration, sometimes its direction, and sometimes its assurance. Sometimes it makes me realize I have to give something up, laying it down so I can pick up my vision. But the more I spend time with God, the more I realize that laying those things down is worth it.

Nothing is Wasted

Can you recall an experience or interaction that you can't seem to forget? It could be positive or negative, but it keeps coming up in your life. For me, I remember a time when I felt like I was being overlooked musically. I complained to God about how things were going, what I expected, and even who I felt overlooked by. In response, I felt like I was supposed to do two things. One was to have a concert called "Beyond the Walls." Two was to write out the phrase "enter-prize thinking."

Long story short, the concert led me into a series of interactions and opportunities. I was privileged to do music with some significant people at the time. I was chosen to be a part of the band for the well-known organization *Promise Keepers*. When I got that part, they showed me a list of everyone else who had been recommended. The list included the *very same people I prayed about months before*!

Years later, while praying about the status of my vision pursuit, and asking about any adjustments I needed to make, I was reminded of the second thing I wrote down that day – "enter-prize" thinking. I started making adjustments to treat myself like an enterprise. No experience I had was wasted, from a list of people I felt overlooked by, to the car accident, to failure after failure, and even my many accomplishments. No part of our stories is wasted, and the keystone moments that keep coming back to our memory, they come up for a reason.

I do want to tread carefully here. I'm not saying that God causes pain, trauma, or misfortune, so they can benefit us in some way later. I know many people ask, "Why do bad things happen to good people?" Or, "Does God allow or cause our suffering?" And my honest answer is, I don't know. However, when I reflect on life, I choose to embrace the thought process that God doesn't waste any of our experiences. He has a way of using them all to get us to where we're going.

Create Space for the Space

On a practical level, there are some things we can do to create space for "the space." Physically, we've talked about the importance of exercise and healthy eating because of its impact on our mental and emotional health. If we're tired, in pain, or hungry, focusing and staying present will feel impossible. Creating physical space can also refer to our physical environment. Do you have a place where you can go to be quiet, uninterrupted, and at peace? Does this place exist in your home?

Maybe for you, time is a factor. You have to go to "the space" early in the morning or late at night while people are sleeping. I know that some people like to have things like pillows and candles in their physical space to help them get to "the space." Everyone is different. You'll have to figure out what works for you.

Another way we create space is with our emotions and mental health. This includes practices like meditation and silence. You can use apps like *Calm* or *Headspace* to assist you. Journaling also helps us free our minds of our current feelings and experiences. In addition to these practices, I am a strong proponent of therapy. It will help you process your thoughts and emotions, particularly with someone unattached from your life and equipped to provide neutral, non-biased support. Finding ways to clear up emotional and mental space will be half the battle.

Lastly, is creating spiritual space, but how do we create space spiritually? Does that look like playing prayer or meditation music, worship songs, or reading and listening to scripture? Maybe not scripture but listening to positive affirmations. Only you really know what you need to enter "the space." If you don't know, embrace the gift of exploration. Be willing to explore the space. There's something more than journeying through life alone. You don't have to handle things in your own strength, or settle for less when difficulty arises.

If It's Not You, Then Who?

Everything I've mentioned in this book boils down to one thing, *you*. I believe that even if you claim you don't know your purpose or don't have a vision for your life, you have an inkling that there's something more for you. The hobbies you enjoy, the problems that bother you, and the dreams you have all hint at it. But if you don't make a move towards your vision, then who will?

The Children of Israel were on the move for forty years, but they only moved in circles. How long are you willing to take? What's the cost of the time you've already taken? I recognize the difficulty that comes with making changes.

It's hard and scary to step into the unknown, but we can't allow comfort to keep us stuck. Comfort is the enemy of legacy.

My hope is that you've found some courage to see past your own self-perceptions and limitations, that you feel empowered to grow and expand your capacity, and that you feel equipped to take action and be account-able. There's a world full of problems in need of answers, so you can't afford to forget your purpose is the solution.

> Comfort is the enemy of legacy.

READY. SET. GO.
(PRACTICAL SUPPORT FOR THE JOURNEY)

READY. SET. GO.

Congrats on making it to the end of the book, but here's where it really all begins for you. Maybe the beginning is starting with discovering what your purpose actually is or writing down a clear vision for your life. Maybe it's releasing old habits, and taking on new ones, or finding a mentor or community that will support and encourage you along the way. Whatever the beginning is for you, my admonishment is that you start now. Why wait? Think about this: how long have you been waiting to live in the fullness of your purpose, to find and create a rhythm that supports your vision, a rhythm that you can actually stick to, and engage in healthy practices and connect with a community that holds you accountable?

These next four mini-chapters are designed to provide practical support for your journey. When I think about vision and purpose and how to practically live it out, I like to break it down into these four categories: Discover Your

Purpose, Map It Out, Encouragement to Act and Harmony to Sustain. You'll find some practical insights, examples, and questions that I hope will be of value to you and your vision.

I know we are all in different spaces, so you don't necessarily have to read these in order. It's kind of like a buffet, take what you want from it. However, I encourage you to really engage beyond just reading. Take time to reflect, answer the questions, watch the videos and put in the work. Anton Chekhov puts it this way, *"Knowledge is of no value unless you put it into practice."*

DISCOVER YOUR PURPOSE

When I talk about discovering your purpose, I'm talking about the reason you are breathing. If someone asked you right now, *"What is your purpose?"* What would you say?

I can't count how many times I've been asked by people of all ages, *"How do I know what my purpose is?"* I get it, it's such a big life question. We all want to know why we are breathing. What is our purpose on earth and how can one be sure?

First, we have to understand that our purpose is not limited to what we do. Think about it: when you were little and people asked, "What do you want to be when you grow up?" the response was typically an occupation. Even as you think about your purpose, maybe the picture you get is tied to what you do. I'd imagine this is where frustration, discontent, and overall conflict arise because I believe purpose is so much greater than what we do to sustain ourselves.

What most people don't consider is that you can operate in your purpose without it being confined to work because your purpose, your way of being, is not solely tied to what you do.

Don't get me wrong, having an occupation, pursuing your dream job, etc., is fine, but living in purpose and on purpose is about the full expression of who you were created to be in everything you do. It's about how you show up in the world, how you interact with others or as some call it, your way of being.

So, the question at hand is, how does one actually go about discovering their purpose? You may need to reexamine and do some more exploration. But either way, this one simple thing will be of great help - ask more questions.

Ask More Questions

American engineer and author William Edwards Deming once said, *"If you do not know how to ask the right question, you discover nothing."* What I've observed over time is people ask the big questions and then stop. Maybe they stop because they're frustrated by uncertainty or lack of clarity or because they think they know and just run with it and don't return.

Whenever I'm coaching people and we're doing exploration around purpose, there's a list of questions I use during the process. The questions can be broken down into the following categories: life experiences, work and play, and passion. While I'm not going to include an extensive list of questions for each, I encourage you to take time to reflect on the questions for yourself, maybe invite friends and family into your inquiry for feedback, or go over some with a mentor, coach, or therapist. I believe the more questions you ask and honestly answer, the closer you will be to discovering your purpose.

Life Experiences

- *What is your favorite childhood memory? Why?*
- *How has your family shaped your thinking?*
- *Have you ever traveled outside of your city? If so, where and what was that like for you?*
- *What is your definition of love? Do you love yourself?*
- *What is your definition of worth? Do you believe you're worth what you want?*
- *Who do you admire the most?*
- *What is the worst thing that has ever happened to you?*

Work and Play

- *What are you good at?*

- *What comes naturally to you?*

- *What do you currently do for work? What do you like or not like about it?*

- *What's your work history?*

- *What do you do for fun?*

- *Do you have any hobbies?*

- *Do you have mentors? What do they do?*

- *What does your schedule look like? Is there time for your vision?*

Passion

- *What would you do for no money?*

- *What do you hate about the world?*

- *What is your biggest distraction?*

- *Is your vision for the world or local?*

- *What dreams did you give up on?*

As you can see, there are so many questions you can ask yourself. Imagine your responses to the questions as dots and as you take time to reflect, hopefully, you will find yourself beginning to connect the dots through patterns and themes. What I've experienced is that when people really take time to trace their life stories and ask deeper questions, they find that clear evidence of their purpose has been there all along.

Decide, Declare, and Do

Even with all the reflection and feedback, you may still find yourself challenged with uncertainty or lack of clarity and that's okay. You may feel like you need to stay in discovery mode and figure it all out before making moves and that's okay too. In a sense, we're all in discovery mode. No matter where we are on this journey, we will always continue to uncover and receive clarity about our purpose. The problem is we can't allow the uncertainty, fear, and trying to gather all the pieces, so to speak, to keep us from moving forward.

If you haven't already come to some conclusion about your purpose, you get to decide what it is. Based on your experiences, your life story, reflection, and feedback, make an educated guess and lean confidently into that. Remember, this isn't completely about what you want to do, but your purpose for existing, the kind of person you want to be, and how you want to show up in the world. Everything will flow from there.

Once you decide, begin to declare it. One of my friends and Session 5 coaches, Ruth Gado Coleman, leads an organization called the Jonah Inheritance that provides solutions to the medical care crises in Nigeria. I love Ruth's personal declaration which is to *"Bring hope and healing to those that are suffering."* Her declaration is not only expressed through the Jonah Inheritance but also in her life commitment.

Even if you can't clearly articulate your purpose, you can still confidently declare that your purpose is the solution!

Lastly, do something! Take a step forward on this journey. A part of your discovery process could look like trying new things. Maybe you've decided or have some sense of your purpose. Now, it's time for the next step – get a new mentor or coach, enroll in a program, start writing a business plan, etc. Don't delay any longer, just do something.

MAP IT OUT

You can't get anywhere you've never been without a map. Maps are designed for guidance, points of reference, and, ultimately, to lead us to our desired destination. That's how I think of vision. You have a destination you are working towards and you need practical directions to get there. Vision is how you live out your purpose, while purpose is what drives your vision. Your commitment to be and do what you see is fueled by the reason you're breathing.

We covered this in Chapter 5 when we talked about overall vision vs. your life vision. Remember your overall vision is the umbrella under which your life operates. It's the overarching vision statement for your life, which includes your purpose declaration. Whereas your life vision guides your day-to-day. It's what you commit to that will move you toward your vision. Your overall vision may expand, and you may need to adjust your life vision as you accomplish goals, reach milestones, or simply as seasons change in your life.

Create Your Own Map

It would be nice if our life vision was more like a GPS than a map. Someone telling us exactly what to do next, the fastest route possible, how to avoid delays and detours, and what to do to get back on track when we make a wrong turn, but that's just not the case. We get to create and follow an old-school map. Luckily, some people have traveled some of the roads we may take, which is why mentors and coaches are key.

So, when you take a look at your overall vision, answer this question: *"What does a person who has this kind of overall vision look like? What are their actions every day?"*

Let's use me as an example. My overall vision states,

*"I, Jonathan DeCuir, am one of the most sought-after voices that God uses to proclaim **wholeness** as His central theme – while encouraging people toward their Kingdom Purpose. Because of this fact, I will influence 1 Million people to pursue their purpose. I will do this by offering outstanding insight, releasing books and inspirational music, and selling my training products, services, and conferences to grow the S5 Visionators inner circle to over 1000 members. I will faithfully execute the brilliant strategies I have received and courageously overcome every single challenge UNTIL my goal has been achieved."*

It sounds great; it includes my purpose and a clear vision, and generally says how I will accomplish it, but what does it actually look like?

When writing your own overall vision, be sure to include the same components as above, your purpose and primary gifting, the problem you want to solve in the world and your overarching life goals. I didn't include some other specific goals and details in my vision statement above, but you can include whatever specific goals or desires you have. The more specific it is, the better.

From there, I wrote down everything I felt like I needed to do to accomplish the vision. I included something for each of the five core areas of life because it would be delusional to think they are not all necessary or they don't all impact each other.

When developing your own life vision, here are some questions you can process in each area to help you create or adjust it:

Physical

- *What is the state of your overall health? Is it compatible or sustainable for your vision?*
- *What does your diet look like? What adjustments do you need to make there?*

- *How often do you exercise? How often would you like to exercise?*

- *What would help you function optimally physically?*

- *How often do you consult with a physician, wellness or holistic doctor, etc.?*

Mental

- *Do you practice meditation or visualization?*

- *How many hours in a day do you watch TV or engage in social media? What impact does that have on you?*

- *How do you continue to learn or grow? (reading, listening to podcasts, etc.)*

- *How often do you see a therapist, counselor, or coach?*

Emotional

- *What do you do for self-care?*

- *How often do you see a therapist or counselor?*

- *Are there any negative habits you need to address? (ex: emotional eating or shopping)*

- *What positive relationships and connections do you have?*

Financial

- *How much money do you save? Do you have a savings goal you're working towards?*

- *What methods do you use to save?*

- *Do you invest your money?*

- *How financially literate are you? What are you doing to learn more?*

Spiritual

- *Do you believe in God? What does your relationship with God currently look like?*

- *Do you pray? Do you read God's word?*

- *What other spiritual practices or disciplines could you incorporate?*

As you map out your vision, be specific. If your life vision is not specific and has no measurement, then you're probably less likely to do it, and how would you know if you are on target? How much are you going to save? How often? What methods will you use? A clear goal could sound like, *"I will save $1000 every month by eating out only on weekends and using the Qaptial app."* Again, you need measurements and methods.

Put It on the Calendar

In addition to being specific, the most important thing we have to do is schedule it. We could all probably attest to saying, *"If it's not on your calendar, then it doesn't exist."* Scheduling your life vision is going to be key to accomplishing it. If you have a job, family, and all the many other responsibilities that come with life, it may be overwhelming to add another thing to the calendar. You may be thinking, I don't even have time to actually sit down and go through this whole process, but I'm going to encourage you, actually challenge you, to make the time. In part, this is the only way you'll be able to accomplish it all. You may need to adjust your schedule at times or be more focused, but the key is simply having a schedule and sticking with it. Remember, *"Pray It, Say It, Schedule It, Do It."* Your overall vision becomes a reality when you choose to live it every day.

If you want additional resources for discovering your purpose and mapping it out, you can sign up for our course "8 Steps to Finding and Pursuing Your God-Given Purpose" by visiting our website session5institute.com.

ENCOURAGEMENT TO ACT

How often do you find yourself in a situation where you know what to do, have all the resources, have been to relevant conferences, and have read all the books but you're still not pursuing your vision or are stuck at a certain goal? Do you know what's holding you back? Is it fear or something else? What kind of encouragement would compel you to move forward?

By definition, encouragement is the "action of giving someone support, confidence, or hope." Ask yourself what you don't ask for support with and why. Are you lacking confidence and what would increase it? Or have you given up hope on a goal or dream? Why?

When I looked a little deeper into the etymology of the word, I found that broken down, en- means "*cause to be*" and courage is connected to your heart and frame of mind. The meaning is further expanded as "*having a quality of mind which enables one to meet danger and trouble without fear."* So, in part, encouragement is an inner reality and it's about having a proper perspective.

We've talked about perception quite a bit, as it is a central theme in the Vision Continuum, so when we find ourselves discouraged, we have to explore what's causing the lack of courage. Do you know where to start? Interestingly enough, in Middle English, courage was mainly used for "what is in one's mind or thoughts" and what better place to begin.

Have you ever taken the time to keep a log of your thoughts, especially the ones you have about yourself, your vision or your goals? What do you tell yourself when opportunity knocks at your door? Do you say, *"I can't do it,"* *"What if I fail,"* or *"I'm not ready?"* Do you have a default thought or feeling that feels safe?

As a practical exercise, I encourage you to create a log of thoughts. Specifically, the negative and discouraging ones that keep you from pursuing your vision in any way. I suggest keeping the log for at least 7 days. Maybe you can create it in the notes section of your phone or a small journal so that you can write down as much as possible. You can also include details like what triggered the thought.

Once you complete a log, review it, and notice what it reveals. Any themes? Do you have a specific thought that is your go-to? Whatever you find, I challenge you to stay aware and curious. I also encourage you to challenge yourself by choosing to think thoughts that are encouraging and empowering you towards your vision.

I love the way the scripture puts it, *"Finally, beloved, whatever is true, whatever is honorable, whatever is just, whatever is pure, whatever is pleasing, whatever is commendable, if there is any excellence and if there is anything worthy of praise, think about these things."* The word *"think"* here means to *"decide"* or *"weigh."* So, you get to decide and allow encouraging, supportive thoughts to have more weight than your default thoughts.

In addition to shifting perspective by changing how we think, encouragement also includes having something outside of ourselves to draw from. The support, confidence, and hope needed can come as a result of building capacity, as well as, connecting with others. No matter what you're doing, capacity and connection are going to be central to your success.

I wrote a book years ago called *How to Fill a Room When No One Knows Your Name*. It is a comprehensive guide for maximizing attendance at your event or concert. While that isn't what we're talking about, some of the principles in the book are relevant to the topic at hand, mainly as it relates to increasing capacity. If you recall, capacity is one of the key tenets of the Vision Continuum and it involves increasing in competence. Competence isn't just about learning more but acting on what you learn. There's a direct correlation between competence and confidence. The more you act, the more you'll be encouraged to act. Kobe said it this way, "confidence comes from preparation."

Ultimately, writing *How to Fill a Room When No One Knows Your Name* came as a result of all the years I spent watching my mentor, performing in concerts, and putting on my own. I developed a level of competency in this area, so much so that I could write a book about it and be confident in my ability to do it with little to no effort. That said, here are 5 practical ways to increase capacity so you have the courage to act.

1. Act courageously

As I said above, the more you act, the more you will be encouraged to act. So, if you've been waiting for a sign or encouragement to do something, here it is. Just Do It! Sometimes, that means you'll have to do it afraid or uncertain, but what matters most is that you do it, whatever the next step of the journey requires.

One of our Session Five Visionator Circle members, Rachelle, has developed a brand and coaching business called "In Courage." She's committed to championing people to live courageously because she believes it's in courage that you find exactly what you need to reach your destination. When telling me about an opportunity she had to speak at a major event, she said, *"People often say no to opportunity or don't take action now because they believe they will not be ready when it's time. Who's to say the process won't equip you? Take the courage to say yes, prepare, and ask for help along the way if needed."*

Question: *What's something you can do now that will require you to say yes courageously?*

2. Be consistent

Consistency is central to building capacity. It's kind of like working out and building your muscles. The more you do it, the more weight you'll be able to lift and the more confident you'll be in your ability to hold it. Consistency will always challenge comfort because it requires you to do things when you don't feel like it.

This is an indicator of belief and growth. When you truly believe in your vision and what's needed to accomplish it, then you'll be compelled to act. Consistency is an indicator of growth because it is the bridge between actions and habits and it's our habits that lead to our dreams. Ask yourself, *where in my life am I lacking consistency and how is it impacting my vision?*

Lastly, what most people don't take into consideration is consistency attracts new people. Social media is a perfect example of this. When content creators are consistent in creating and posting, more people tend to engage, like, and share their content. When you are consistent, someone new and unexpected may notice and be willing to support you and your vision. Consistency may be the key to unlocking the door you least expect.

3. Connect to a cause

When you connect to a cause that's bigger than you, it connects your vision to something bigger than your sphere of influence. It also gives your vision intent and makes you focus on something outside of yourself. Others will be compelled to support and participate because they're able to see how your vision is tangibly connected to a bigger cause. For example, my connection to the Jonah Inheritance and participation in their medical missions' trips invited others to not only support S5 and the 'My Purpose is the Solution' campaign, but also indirectly impact all the people I'd encounter in Nigeria.

Is there a cause in your local community or globally that you can connect with? Even if it's a short-term partnership, this will allow you to act in your vision while also expanding your capacity and influence.

4. Collaborate with others

When you're building capacity, you don't have to do it all by yourself. In fact, I'd argue you can't. Collaboration opens up more possibilities to learn, grow, and be exposed to new opportunities and connections. Remember, vision is bigger than you, so collaboration allows both your vision and the vision of who you're collaborating with to impact more people with less effort.

Collaboration can also look like leveraging the credibility of someone you're connected to. However, I suggest this is something you don't overuse or do without permission. Leveraging someone else's credibility for your vision can look like using their name and influence to increase your own credibility. It may give you access to people and resources you might not have had otherwise. This type of collaboration is a gift and should be used wisely.

Take a moment, yes right now, to write down the names of 5 people you can collaborate with in the next 6 months. What are you hoping to accomplish with each of them?

5. Engage in community

I will always be an advocate for surrounding oneself with like-minded people. Napoleon Hill said it best, *"Deliberately seek the company of people who influence you to think and act on building the life you desire."* Having mentors and coaches are essential, but you also need a community of people who you can relate with, and who are just as committed as you are to this journey. I am not asking you to disregard people who are not "on your level," but having people who share a common vision of living a life of purpose, and who can support and challenge you is important.

Before Napoleon Hill, there was Jesus. He even had a mastermind group. He gathered 12 people around Him from very different walks of life to journey with Him as He lived out his purpose and pursued the vision God gave Him. He refused to do it alone. While Jesus did most of the investment, encouragement, and accountability, I guarantee the human side of Him felt glad to have people with Him. I bet the disciples made it easier for Him to choose to stay the course and fulfill His mission.

I've experienced firsthand the impact of participating in a mastermind. You wouldn't be reading this book if not for the encouragement and accountability I received from the guys I met with faithfully for a year.

In the words of motivational speaker Jim Rohn, *"You are the average of the five people you spend the most time with."* I'd put it this way: your inner circle, with whom you engage in community, is a reflection of your future. That said, I want to challenge you to take a survey of who you surround yourself with. What kind of lifestyle do they have? What do their finances or health look like? How are they pursuing their vision?

HARMONY TO SUSTAIN

We've all witnessed someone reaching heightened success or finally obtaining their vision, only to find themselves in some sort of personal trouble. Whether it's addiction of some sort, poor financial decisions, relationship drama, or full-on spiraling out of control to their demise. Think of all the musicians, celebrity artists, Hollywood actors and actresses, major CEOs and executives that have been in the headlines for the things I mentioned above. Even the greats aren't exempted: Michael Jackson, Whitney Houston, Prince, and the list goes on, simply because they couldn't balance it all. They may have been thriving in their careers, exceeding their goals and dreams, but many were troubled by other significant areas of their life that needed their attention or even further development.

I mentioned early on in the book that vision is a chisel. If we allow it, it will sculpt us not only into who we're destined to be but the kind of person we need to be for the vision to materialize. Some people may obtain their vision but lack the character to sustain it. This occurs more often than not because the focus is only on doing what is needed to reach the vision, not what will keep one there once they arrive.

Trying to maintain balance over seeking harmony will always lead to frustration and failure because balance implies that everything gets equal weight, which is unrealistic. Life simply isn't set up that way. Most of the time, when people talk about a need for balance in life, they simply want to juggle between things, not actively find a way to make all that's necessary work together.

When I talk about harmony, I mean all the parts playing together at the same time. As a musician and music producer, I value good harmony because it adds life and fullness to the sound of the song. By definition, *"harmony is a combination of tones pleasing to the ear."* The root of the words means *agreement* or *to fit together.*[13] So, harmony happens in our lives when what we believe, say, and do are all in agreement with our vision. More specifically, it's when the physical, mental, emotional, financial, and spiritual aspects of our lives fit together. When they are all uniquely working on one accord, not one over or without another. I think this is where we get in trouble because we believe that our choices and actions in one area of our life will impact others.

To assess whether you're operating in harmony, simply take some time to do some life inventory. Are you reaching your life vision goals? What areas are being left behind or neglected altogether? Do you know why that's the case? Are you moving towards or living in your vision, but notice some questionable things about your character? What kind of shifts do you need to make? Harmony will not make everything easier, but it will support and sustain you.

As we know, vision acts as a destination and the map for getting us there. It gives us reason to be disciplined and dedicated, but we still have to be discerning of the seasons of our lives. What I mean is that practicing harmony requires that we are intentional and attentive. In the God section of Vision Continuum, I mentioned the ability to notice when inspiration comes, but the ability to notice is also needed here. Practically, do you notice the cues your body gives you for what it needs? Are you mindful of your spending and saving habits? What about your emotional and mental state? What do you notice there?

Yes, this is what having a life vision is for, creating goals and practices for all of these areas, but we still have to be aware of present needs that arise and prepare for what's coming. Do you have an action plan for the unexpected or the future?

Sometimes we need additional support and resources to help us. Here are some questions you can process as you practice harmony:

- Would you benefit from a physical trainer, coach, or therapist in this season?

- Do you have an up-to-date Trust and Last Will?

- When was the last time you did a full health exam? Would you benefit from visiting a holistic doctor?

- What's something new you could learn more about to support your vision?

From the Vision Continuum to habits to mapping out our life vision, this book is full of information and questions to process as we pursue vision. To support you in maintaining harmony, I encourage you to go through the book as often as needed to engage with the information. Continue to build capacity, be inspired by God, be accountable, and most importantly, challenge and shift your perception.

Ultimately, it all comes down to belief. Whether we choose to believe it or not, we all have a purpose and it is the solution. So, go, live in purpose and on purpose.

10 Quick Tips for Pursuing Your Vision

Here are 10 quick tips and overviews for pursuing your vision. Feel free to review them when needed and share them with others who you know need a little jump start on their journey.

1. Determine your overall vision vs. life vision

Your overall vision is what you're ultimately working toward. Your life vision is how you will get there. Develop routines and habits that support you in reaching your vision instead of hindering you.

2. Write your vision down

I often say writing down your vision is one of the fastest manifestations of God. If you've been given a vision, the first step to seeing it is putting it on paper.

3. Grow in self-awareness

Take time to pay attention to your thoughts, your internal self-talk, and your behaviors. This may require you to be vulnerable and invite others into the process for feedback. Since we live in our bodies, we can't always see ourselves. We need a mirror and that could sometimes be the people in our lives.

4. Develop a schedule

People and things will always demand our time and attention. It's important to schedule time to learn, work, and rest. Once we develop a schedule, stick to it.

5. Get a mentor

I can't stress the significance of mentors enough. Mentors may help us save time and money and reduce mistakes. When we humble ourselves and open up to learning, we may receive more than we anticipated.

6. Make investments

You have to invest in yourself and your vision. When you spend money on learning or growing and enhancing our business, don't view it as an expense, but rather an investment. Which means you should expect a return.

7. Join an accountability group

Joining an accountability group or mastermind is a great way to keep you moving toward your vision. You receive support, and feedback. It's also a great way to change your references. You are able to engage with like-minded people or people you aspire to be like one day. You might find the group I help run called the Session 5 Institute (S5i) right up your alley. You can learn more at https://www.session5institute.com/.

8. Adjust your environment to support your vision

This simply means creating an environment or space where you can be inspired to work on your vision. This could be a room in your house, a desk, or simply a wall dedicated to quotes and affirmations. You can also use things like vision boards or some other tangible representation that will motivate you every day.

9. Honor the journey

Sometimes we get so caught up in the ups and downs of life that we lose sight of the goal. We forget that the point of the journey is to help us get to where we are going, which includes all the "good" and "bad" things we experience along the way. When you honor the journey, you choose to embrace all that comes with it, knowing it is all being used as a chisel to turn you into a masterpiece.

10. **Just start somewhere**

The hardest part for most people is starting. It's starting the book, starting the business, joining the group, but starting somewhere is a good first step. Starting for you could look like having a conversation with someone who could help you get on the right track. It could be as simple as writing down the title and table of contents for your book or drafting a simple business plan. Just start somewhere. Thankfully, you don't have to figure it all out alone.

NO ONE WALKS ALONE

Now What: A Note from Jon

Whenever people read a book or receive information, normally the next question asked is "now what"? Sometimes, I think we use that question as a way to evade responsibility. If we act like we don't know what to do, then it's likely we won't do anything. If we're honest, we know exactly what to do. You know exactly what to do next. This book is filled with tons of next steps and action items.

I want to encourage you to go back and review your reflections and notes. Create an action plan for your life and how you plan to actively pursue your purpose.

If I haven't learned anything over the last 2 decades of doing this work, I have learned that no one walks alone. This journey of pursuing vision is personal, but it doesn't have to be lonely. I cannot reiterate it enough: find a group of people, a coach, or a mentor who can support you along the way.

About the Author

Jonathan DeCuir, M.Div. is a multifaceted leader and visionary committed to impacting lives through dynamic preaching, speaking, coaching, and leadership. With over 20 years of experience, a wealth of knowledge, and wisdom, Jon has been known to inspire people across religious, political, and cultural boundaries. Jon is a native of Pasadena, CA, where he currently serves as the Lead Pastor at Victory Bible Church. In addition to his role as pastor, Jon is also an author, vision coach, community leader, mentor and scholar. His unique ability to cast vision, effectively communicate complex ideas, and empower individuals to act beyond limitations is the fruit of his faithfulness to God and dedication to hard work. Among his many endeavors and accomplishments, Jon's greatest feat and joy is being the best father he can to his son Noah.

Visit www.jondecuir.com to find out more.

About Session 5 Institute

Session 5 Institute is a non-profit organization founded by Jon DeCuir. It began over 20 years as *Vision 5*, a group created to help people obtain their vision by transforming the five key areas of life, (physical, mental, emotional, spiritual, and financial). It evolved into Session 5, offering dynamic church service experiences and mentoring. As it continued to evolve, the institute added more services, like accountability groups, courses, resources, and one-on-one coaching. It has served people around the globe, helping them to discover their purpose, be inspired to dream again, and actively pursue their vision.

Learn more about the Session 5 Institute and all that it offers at www.session5institute.com

Acknowledgments

One of the things that I have learned over the years is this: I can't accomplish anything without the support of an amazing team of people. This journey has been both challenging and rewarding at the same time. I learned the value of finishing and the value of presence. I started this journey with a group of people, not knowing that my very dear friend and brother Donald would not be here to celebrate this accomplishment with me. I'm sure the rest of the team would agree – the time that we spent together was priceless.

Thank you! To Leslie Calum, our original scribe, for getting this book to a point where we could read it. To Jennifer Nicholas of *Buried Treasures*, another scribe and interpreter that got us over the hump, one who always pushes for excellence. To Melendy Butler, the scribe who always finds ways for people to engage with the material. To Donald Pearson, another scribe and the argumentative debater who always made us work through the issues. To Deji Olajide, for researching and helping us refine. To Quanesha Moore, the scribe who brought us to the finish line and streamlined the work. You guys are the best team anyone could ask for. The reward was truly the journey. I can't help but wish that we could re-live some of those moments just to be able to spend more time with our brother Donald. I know that this accomplishment is making you smile, bro.

To my hero, my mother, Linda DeCuir, thank you mom for always using the power of words to make me believe that I was special, and that I would change the world. Thank you for letting me see YOU before you transitioned. You made me realize that there would be people who, like you, are amazing with more to give, but need a little tug. I am committed to pulling greatness out of everyone that I see who has your look in their eyes, mom. Wish I knew then what I know now, so I could have helped you more.

I want to thank my dad for giving me a legacy to follow. Your drive and commitment to your calling is unprecedented. I love you, dad. It's an honor and joy to walk in your footsteps, and as my own son grows up, it makes me appreciate everything you did for me all the more.

To my mentors who pushed me along this journey. Special shout-out to Evan for making me accountable to get this done. Thank you for calling me forward and not letting me off the hook. Sometimes it's easy not to "drink your own juice." I'm thankful that I have mentors who push me to buy what I sell to others.

To all of my family and friends who have been there for me through the years – I love all of you guys. Thank you for believing in me.

Last but not least, to my son – I am hoping that one day, you will read this as my footprints in the sand for you to follow. Son, I urge you to learn from my mistakes and my successes. Let these footprints lead you and guide you to your own "Promised Land." Love you to life.

Notes

1   Luke 2:52

2   Noel Burch, an employee with Gordon Training International, developed the Conscious Competence Ladder in the 1970s. The model highlights two factors that affect our thinking as we learn a new skill: consciousness (awareness) and skill level (competence).

3   Quote by Stephen Covey,

4   Ray Dalio quote

5   n his book Outliers: The Story of Success

6   Gap Community information

7   https://www.psychologytoday.com/us/blog/the-power-prime/201908/perception-is-not-reality

8   Who is steven richards

9   About neil and truth

10 https://www.etymonline.com/word/intention

11 Proverbs 12:1 amp

12 Bessel A. van der Kolk, The Body Keeps the Score: Brain, Mind, and Body in the Healing of Trauma

13 https://www.etymonline.com/word/harmony#etymonline_v_6172 (harmony to sustain quote)